The
Green
Year

365 small things you can do
to make a **big** difference

Jodi Helmer

ALPHA

A member of Penguin Group (USA) Inc.

ALPHA BOOKS

Published by the Penguin Group

Penguin Group (USA) Inc., 375 Hudson Street, New York, New York 10014, USA

Penguin Group (Canada), 90 Eglinton Avenue East, Suite 700, Toronto, Ontario M4P 2Y3, Canada (a division of Pearson Penguin Canada Inc.)

Penguin Books Ltd, 80 Strand, London WC2R 0RL, England

Penguin Ireland, 25 St. Stephen's Green, Dublin 2, Ireland (a division of Penguin Books Ltd.)

Penguin Group (Australia), 250 Camberwell Road, Camberwell, Victoria 3124, Australia (a division of Pearson Australia Group Pty. Ltd.)

Penguin Books India Pvt. Ltd., 11 Community Centre, Panchsheel Park, New Delhi—110 017, India

Penguin Group (NZ), 67 Apollo Drive, Rosedale, North Shore, Auckland 1311, New Zealand (a division of Pearson New Zealand Ltd.)

Penguin Books (South Africa) (Pty.) Ltd, 24 Sturdee Avenue, Rosebank, Johannesburg 2196, South Africa

Penguin Books Ltd., Registered Offices: 80 Strand, London WC2R 0RL, England

International Standard Book Number: 978-1-59257-829-0
Library of Congress Catalog Card Number: 2008929023

10   09   08   8   7   6   5   4   3   2   1

Interpretation of the printing code: The rightmost number of the first series of numbers is the year of the book's printing; the rightmost number of the second series of numbers is the number of the book's printing. For example, a printing code of 08-1 shows that the first printing occurred in 2008.

Printed in the United States of America

For Charlotte, who deserves to grow up in a great, green world.

Introduction

Making changes in our own lives to be more environmentally friendly is one of the most important things we can do for the planet. But what does it mean to live green, and where do you start?

The Green Year is about making small changes—such as switching light bulbs, turning down the thermostat, and choosing natural cleaning products—to protect the environment. You don't have to purchase a bunch of expensive equipment or embark on monthlong projects to overhaul your entire life. By making one small change, one day at a time, you can have a huge effect on the planet.

The book contains 365 simple and inexpensive tips to help you become more eco-friendly. The tips are organized by date, making it easy to find green living tips for any time of the year: flip to April for ideas on greening your garden or turn to November for ideas on planning an environmentally friendly Thanksgiving celebration.

You can try all of the tips or pick and choose the ones that best suit your lifestyle. Be sure to check off the things you've tried and write in suggestions or modifications that worked best for you.

Have fun—and remember, little changes do add up!

Acknowledgments

I spent months researching and writing *The Green Year*, but it was not a solo project. I could not have written a single page of this book (or anything for that matter) without the support of my family and an amazing group of friends and freelancers cheering me on.

I owe a huge debt of gratitude to my parents, Hank and Dianne Helmer, for encouraging my passion for writing—and for the midafternoon calls to make sure that I was eating *and* writing. I am especially indebted to Eric Eckard, a rock-star researcher and amazing friend, for listening to my stress-induced rants and talking me down from the ledge (again), and the Freelance Support Hos for saying the right things at the right times, providing editing suggestions, and sending chocolate in the mail. I'm also grateful to Marilyn Allen, my indefatigable agent, who came to me with this project; and Michele Wells, my editor at Alpha Books, for taking a chance on a first-time author. While I was on deadline for *The Green Year*, Greg Betz reminded me that writing a book is like eating an elephant; it's best done one step at a time. It's advice that kept me pounding away at the keyboard, even when it was 3 A.M.

My final, and most heartfelt, thank you is to Jeff Paramchuk, for giving me the courage to write.

January 1

Recycle your Christmas tree.

Christmas trees can be ground into woodchips and used as fragrant mulch in your garden or spread at a local watershed to prevent erosion. Rent a wood chipper with a neighbor or two and make your own mulch. Or go to www.earth911.org and enter your zip code to find out where to have your tree recycled.

An alternative to this idea that works better for me is:

_____

_____

January 2

Replace your furnace filter.

You can help keep your heating system operating at maximum efficiency by changing the filters every month during peak operating season.

Clogged filters reduce airflow through the heating and cooling system, reducing energy efficiency. Installing a new furnace filter can also help reduce airborne allergens like dust, pollen, and mold. For most furnaces it's a very simple process: just slide the old one out and the new one in. Check your owner's manual.

Filters come in several different sizes, so be sure to take the measurements when you go shopping. Some disposable furnace filters cost under $10 and can often be purchased at home improvement centers and in the hardware aisle of the local supermarket.

An alternative to this idea that works better for me is:

_____

_____

January 3

Seal the leaks in your attic.

A leaky attic can make the whole house feel cold and damp. Plugging any leaks in the attic prevents heat from escaping out of the house, saving resources and money. In the attic, look for any obvious holes and feel around for leaks. Use caulking and foam to seal the leaks. You might also consider adding extra insulation in the attic to help retain heat during the winter months.

An alternative to this idea that works better for me is:

_____

_____

January 4

Improve your water heater's efficiency by adding insulation.

Insulating your water heater can reduce heat loss by up to 45 percent. Home improvement centers sell insulating blankets in one size for under $20. To maximize energy efficiency, choose a blanket with an insulating value of at least R-8.

It's easy to install an insulating blanket on an electric water heater. Take the blanket out of the package, wrap it around your water heater (pretend you're wrapping a cylindrical birthday present), and cut it to fit. Just make sure that the insulation does not extend past the top of the water heater, as this could be a safety hazard. Leave the thermostat panel uncovered and be sure the temperature is not set above 130 degrees (otherwise the wiring may overheat).

It is significantly more difficult to install an insulating blanket on a gas- or oil-fired water heater, so it's best to call a qualified plumbing or heating contractor.

An alternative to this idea that works better for me is:

_____

_____

January 5

Buy an LED flashlight for emergencies.

Flashlights that use light-emitting diodes (LEDs) produce a strong white light using 90 percent less energy than a traditional bulb and last up to 50 percent longer. Unlike traditional bulbs, LEDs contain no glass casing or filament so there is no chance of the bulb breaking. You can rest easy knowing that your flashlight will work in case of an emergency.

An alternative to this idea that works better for me is:

January 6

Turn down the thermostat.

You'll reduce CO_2 emissions and save about 1 percent on your heating bill for each degree you turn down the temperature over an eight-hour period.

Set the thermostat at 68 degrees when you're at home. It's safe to turn the heat down to 55 degrees at night and during the day when you're at work, as long as you don't have pets that are sensitive to the cold. (Don't turn it down any lower or your pipes might freeze.)

An alternative to this idea that works better for me is:

_____

_____

January 7

Install a programmable thermostat.

If you've already turned down the thermostat to 68 degrees, a programmable thermostat is one of the easiest ways to lower energy use and reduce heating bills.

Programmable thermostats are sold at home improvement centers and hardware stores. Prices start at $50 for a simple unit with a timer. Most are easy to install if you're handy. If you're not, make a quick call to the heating and cooling professionals. It's not a time-consuming job, so it shouldn't cost you an arm and a leg.

Set the thermostat to turn the heat back at night and during the day when you're at work. You can set it to start warming the house back up a half hour before you get up or return home, so the house will be cozy when you need it to be.

An alternative to this idea that works better for me is:
_____
_____

January 8

Close your fireplace damper.

There is nothing more inviting than a crackling fire on a cold winter night. To prevent heat escaping up the chimney when your fireplace is not in use, keep the damper (also called a flue) closed. (But don't forget to open the damper before starting a fire!)

Keeping the damper open is like keeping a window wide open in the winter. Once the damper is closed, make sure it fits snugly. If you can feel a draft, it might be time to replace the damper.

An alternative to this idea that works better for me is:

_____

_____

January 9

Install a low-flow showerhead.

You can eliminate the guilt over taking a steaming hot shower by reducing the amount of water you're using. It only takes a few minutes (and a few dollars) to minimize water usage and save up to 10 percent on your water heating costs.

Replacing your showerhead is as simple as screwing off the old one and screwing on a new one. A simple low-flow showerhead can cost as little as $10 at a home improvement center. Look for showerheads with a flow rate of less than 2.5 gpm (gallons per minute) for maximum efficiency.

Not sure if you already have a low-flow showerhead? Place a bucket—marked in gallon increments—under the showerhead. Turn on the shower and see how long it takes to reach the 1 gallon mark. If it takes less than 20 seconds, it's time to install a low-flow showerhead.

An alternative to this idea that works better for me is:

_____

_____

January 10

Load your dishwasher for maximum efficiency.

Before starting your dishwasher, check that dishes don't block the detergent dispenser or spray arms. Know what makes up an ideal load, so you don't over- or underload. Read the owner's manual to find out how much (or how little) detergent you should use, to eliminate the need for a second wash.

From now on, instead of turning on the dishwasher every night, save energy by running it only when it's full. Allow dishes to air dry, instead of using the heated drying function, to further cut down on energy use.

An alternative to this idea that works better for me is:

_____

_____

January 11

Check the pressure on your car's tires.

Correct tire inflation will increase gas mileage and extend the life of your tires. As a bonus, it will improve your vehicle's handling performance.

To find out how many PSI (pounds per square inch) the manufacturer recommends for your car, check the owner's manual or the inflation sticker found on the driver's doorjamb.

It's best to check your tires when they're cold, but if you don't have an air-pressure gauge, take your car to a gas station and use the gauge on its air pump. (Let the car sit so your tires can cool down.) While you're there, add air to any under-inflated tires. (Make sure your tires are inflated with air; some newer models are inflated with nitrogen.) Be careful not to overinflate.

On average, you should check your tire pressure at least once a month. It's a good idea to check more often in the winter months; tires will lose about 1 PSI for every 10 degrees the temperature drops.

An alternative to this idea that works better for me is:

_____

_____

January 12

Check your car's owner's manual to find out how much warm-up time your car needs to run properly when temperatures are below freezing. (Most need just 30 seconds.) Adjust your schedule to avoid warming up the car longer while you take care of last-minute tasks.

During the cold weather, it might be tempting to let the car run and blast the heater before you get in. Keep in mind that you're burning fuel while your car sits in the driveway, reducing your fuel economy to zero miles per gallon. Letting the car run unattended is also one of the main causes of winter car theft, so this is a good habit to break.

An alternative to this idea that works better for me is:

_____

_____

January 13

Turn your computer off at the end of the day.

Over the course of one year, powering down your computer will save one ton of carbon dioxide emissions. To save even more energy, use the Sleep mode feature on your computer during the day. On a PC, go to the Start menu, click Control Panel, and look for the icon labeled Power Options. There will be a tab labeled Hibernate that will set your computer to automatically power down when it's not in use. On a Mac, go to the Apple tab and click on "sleep" to put your computer in sleep mode.

> The U.S. Department of Energy recommends turning off the monitor if you'll be away from the computer for more than 20 minutes.

An alternative to this idea that works better for me is:

January 14

Look around your house to see if you have any old cell phones that could be recycled or donated to a shelter. Ask your family and friends, too—most people probably have an old cell phone or two lying around.

Cell phones contain mercury, cadmium, lead, and other poisonous materials. If they're tossed into the landfill, these toxic metals will leak into the ground water and could poison streams, wildlife, and drinking water.

> According to the Environmental Protection Agency, there are up to 130 million unused cell phones in the United States. Recycling those phones would save enough energy to power 194,000 households for one year!

Go to www.electronicsrecycling.net and enter your zip code to find out where to recycle your cell phone.

An alternative to this idea that works better for me is:

_____

_____

January 15

Turn off the tap!

You can save 10 gallons of water every morning by simply turning off the tap when you're brushing your teeth, washing your face, or shaving.

An alternative to this idea that works better for me is:
_____
_____

January 16

Unplug your toaster!

Like other appliances in your home, your toaster draws power simply because it's plugged in. It's called standby power or vampire power (because it sucks energy in the middle of the night) and it accounts for 5 percent of residential energy use, costing U.S. consumers over $4 billion per year. To cut your use of standby power, unplug appliances such as toasters, electric can openers, and hairdryers when they're not in use.

An alternative to this idea that works better for me is:

_____

_____

January 17

Take a shower instead of a bath.

The frigid temperatures make a hot bath sound so soothing, but it takes a lot of water to fill the tub. A seven-minute shower with a low-flow showerhead uses approximately 14 gallons of water, while it takes at least 20 gallons of water to fill the bathtub.

Replacing one bath a week with a shower will help a family of four save more than 300 gallons of water per year.

If you must take a bath, plug the tub immediately, adjusting the temperature while it fills to avoid losing water down the drain. To save energy (and feel even more relaxed!) turn off the lights and bathe by candlelight.

An alternative to this idea that works better for me is:

_____

_____

January 18

Call your energy company to research alternative power availability. Instead of relying on nonrenewable energy sources like oil and natural gas, many municipalities are developing eco-friendly energy sources such as solar and wind power. For just a few dollars more per month, you can sign up for an alternative energy program—and a portion of your monthly bill will go toward funding energy sources that will safeguard against depleting resources.

If your energy company doesn't offer alternative power, write them a letter letting them know that it's important to you.

An alternative to this idea that works better for me is:
_____
_____

January 19

Toss your synthetic kitchen sponge and buy a sponge made from cellulose fibers instead.

Synthetic sponges are made from nonrenewable resources and are often soaked in chemicals like triclosan that have antibacterial and antimicrobial properties. Triclosan is also a pesticide that could destroy aquatic life. Triclosan is one of the most common manmade chemicals found in our rivers and streams.

Cellulose fiber comes from recycled wood pulp and is fully biodegradable. They're also much longer lasting than synthetic sponges. Look for cellulose sponges in the cleaning products aisle of any supermarket.

An alternative to this idea that works better for me is:

_____

_____

January 20

Clean your refrigerator coils.

The coils hold liquid that cools the air inside the refrigerator. It takes a lot more energy to cool the refrigerator when the coils are covered with lint and dust. Refrigerator coils should be cleaned at least twice a year.

Pull the refrigerator out from the wall. Vacuum out all the dust, and then wipe down the coils with a damp cloth. In just a few minutes, you can cut your refrigerator's energy use by up to 6 percent!

An alternative to this idea that works better for me is:

_____

_____

January 21

Research energy-efficient appliances to see if they're a good option for your home.

Consider this: an energy-efficient refrigerator uses 75 percent less energy than a refrigerator made in the 1970s.

If you're thinking about replacing or upgrading your appliances, look for brands with an Energy Star label. Energy Star is a government program that certifies energy-efficient products to help consumers make smart purchasing decisions. Energy-efficient appliances might cost more initially but will save you money—and safeguard the environment—in the long run.

To cut costs, look for rebate programs. Many government bodies and energy providers have developed rebate programs to create incentives for buying energy-efficient products. Start your search by visiting www.energystar.gov.

An alternative to this idea that works better for me is:

January 22

Collect your reusable shopping bags and store them in your car.

The next time you're at the supermarket, you'll have the bags with you (no more forgetting them at home). Reusable shopping bags help cut down on waste and preserve natural resources. In the United States, we use 11 million plastic shopping bags every *hour*—that's a lot of waste!

Be sure to ask about rebates for bringing your own bags. Some supermarkets will take 5 cents off of your bill for every bag you bring.

An alternative to this idea that works better for me is:

January 23

Ask your mechanic to recycle your used oil filter.

The next time you take your car to have the oil changed, ask the mechanic to recycle the used oil filter. If you change the oil yourself, be sure to properly dispose of the used oil and oil filter. Call your local waste management company for details on proper disposal in your area.

An alternative to this idea that works better for me is:

January 24

Watch your speed as you drive.

On your way to work this morning, drive the posted speed limit; it's a more eco-friendly choice—and it'll help you avoid a ticket. Fuel economy peaks at 55 mph and begins to drop dramatically when you drive over 60 mph. Increasing your speed by 10 mph decreases fuel efficiency by 5 mpg.

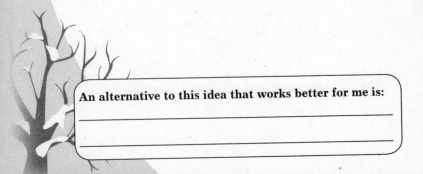

An alternative to this idea that works better for me is:

January 25

Research options for carpooling.

Instead of driving alone, share a ride with a co-worker or ask a neighbor to take turns shuttling the kids to school. You'll save on gas and help reduce your carbon footprint.

Put up a flyer at work to see if others in your office are interested in carpooling, check out local ride-share programs online, or post a message about carpooling on your local community website. You can also call your local transit agency to ask about resources for carpoolers. Many agencies offer free parking at pick-up/drop-off locations and some even help match carpoolers who have similar routes.

An alternative to this idea that works better for me is:
_____
_____

January 26

Tighten your car's gas cap.

If your gas cap is too loose, fuel will evaporate from the gas tank. In the United States, 147 million gallons of gas evaporate every year from cars with gas caps that are damaged, loose, or missing. Make sure your gas cap is tight by turning it until it clicks three times—it's a good habit to get into every time you fill up.

An alternative to this idea that works better for me is:

_____

_____

January 27

Join a carbon-offset program.

Every time you turn on the TV, switch on the lights, or start your car, you emit carbon dioxide into the atmosphere. You can offset your CO_2 emissions by joining a carbon-offset program, such as TerraPass, NativeEnergy, or Carbonfund.org. First, go to www.carbonfootprint.com to calculate your CO_2 emissions (also called your carbon footprint). Carbon-offset programs will, for a small fee, invest in activities to remove an equal amount of carbon from the air.

> Carbon-dioxide emissions are a major contributor to global warming. The average American is responsible for 10 tons of CO_2 emissions annually.

You can also offset your carbon emissions on your next flight with airlines such as Delta and Continental. A round-trip flight from New York to San Francisco emits approximately .77 tons of CO_2. Programs start at $10 and allow passengers to choose one of several carbon-offset options, including international reforestation programs.

Don't forget that you can also reduce your carbon footprint by using energy-efficient light bulbs, recycling aluminum cans, and turning off the lights when you leave a room!

An alternative to this idea that works better for me is:

_____

_____

January 28

Check your office for any old computer equipment you might have lying around.

Donating your old computer is a much better option than tossing it in the trash. More than 1.5 billion pounds of electronics equipment end up in landfills every year, leaking toxic heavy metals like lead and mercury into the soil and water.

Recycling centers will ensure that used computers are disposed of properly. You can also donate your old computer to a nonprofit organization that will refurbish it and donate it to a school or charity in need of computers. Find out where to recycle your computer at www.eiae.org.

An alternative to this idea that works better for me is:

January 29

Create a weekly meal plan that limits red meat to twice a week.

You can dramatically reduce your carbon footprint by replacing red meat with more sustainable options. It takes a significant amount of energy to grow feed for livestock and process red meat. Cattle also produce methane, a greenhouse gas linked to global warming. Instead of steak, choose line-caught fish or experiment with vegetarian dishes.

When you do purchase red meat, support sustainable farming practices by choosing products that are labeled "organic," "free range," and "grass fed."

An alternative to this idea that works better for me is:
_____
_____

January 30

Choose the cold cycle on your washing machine when you're doing a load of laundry.

Roughly 90 percent of the energy consumed by your washing machine is used to heat the water. Choosing the "cold" setting uses significantly less energy and is just as effective as hot water for getting your clothes clean. There are several brands of detergent on the market made specifically for use in cold water.

There are exceptions: some stubborn stains may only be removed with hot water, and bed linens need to be washed on the highest temperature setting to kill dust mites.

An alternative to this idea that works better for me is:

January 31

Make a list of organic foods to try.

On your next trip to the grocery store, add a few organic options to your cart. Organic produce is grown with natural fertilizer and fewer pesticides than its non-organic counterparts. In the United States, produce with the USDA-certified organic label is at least 95 percent organic. The environmental benefits range from keeping chemicals from polluting groundwater to providing a healthy environment for local wildlife. There is also another benefit to choosing organic fruits and vegetables: a lot of people believe they taste better than produce grown with chemical fertilizers.

Always wash your produce before eating it, even if you've purchased organic varieties, because it could contain residual pesticides on its skin.

Organic produce is often more expensive. If you want to buy organic but also want to stick to a budget, it's important to know which fruits and vegetables are most likely to be contaminated by pesticides: apples, apricots, cherries, grapes, nectarines, peaches, raspberries, strawberries, celery, green beans, peppers, and spinach.

An alternative to this idea that works better for me is:
_____
_____

February 1

Research hybrid rental cars for your next vacation.

Companies like Enterprise Rent-a-Car, National Car Rental, and Hertz have a fleet of eco-friendly vehicles in select markets across the country. On average, driving a hybrid vehicle instead of a conventional automobile improves fuel economy by 45 percent. Hybrid vehicles also emit less carbon dioxide, carbon monoxide, and nitrogen oxide, the gas that contributes to depletion of ground-level ozone.

A growing number of car-rental agencies have also launched programs that allow you to offset your carbon emissions. The program costs $1.25 per rental and goes toward certified offset programs that remove carbon dioxide from the atmosphere.

An alternative to this idea that works better for me is:
_____
_____

February 2

Research green hotels for your spring-break getaway.

The Green Hotels Association (www.greenhotels.com) has a comprehensive list of hotels in every state that have implemented programs to conserve resources and reduce waste.

During check-in, request that sheets and towels be changed only if they're left on the floor and leave a note for the housekeeping staff asking that the heat or air conditioning be turned off when you're not in the room. At the end of your stay, fill out the comment card to let management know you appreciate their efforts to be green.

An alternative to this idea that works better for me is:
_____
_____

February 3

Remove your name from catalog mailing lists.

A whopping 8 million tons of trees are used yearly in the production of paper catalogs. You can keep unwanted mail from piling up by going to www.catalogchoice.org and unsubscribing from mailing lists. It's a free service that has a huge environmental impact.

You can continue receiving catalogs from your favorite retailers; just be sure to recycle them when you're finished with them.

An alternative to this idea that works better for me is:

February 4

Install insulated electrical outlet plates.

Drafts seep in though your electrical outlets and let heat escape. Insulated electrical outlet plates are simple to install—just unscrew the existing outlet cover and replace it with the new cover—and cost less than $2 at home improvement stores. It's a small change that will improve energy efficiency.

An alternative to this idea that works better for me is:

_____

_____

February 5

Donate your old bridesmaid dresses.

You might never wear the powder pink strapless gown again, but it could be the perfect prom dress for a teenage girl. The Princess Project collects like-new formal wear and distributes gowns to prom-going teens in the San Francisco area who can't afford to buy new dresses. You can ship your gown to their office (go to www.princessproject.org for guidelines) to help make a girl feel like a princess for a night, and keep your fancy frock from going to the landfill. Currently, clothing makes up 4 percent of the waste found in landfills—a figure that's growing quickly!

An alternative to this idea that works better for me is:

_____

_____

February 6

Replace your old toothbrush with an eco-friendly model.

Your dentist will tell you to replace your toothbrush four times a year—but that means a lot of toothbrushes end up in the garbage. In fact, toothbrushes account for 50 million pounds of trash in U.S. landfills every year. The handles of most toothbrushes are made from nonrenewable petroleum sources and are not biodegradable. Rest assured that you can protect the environment and your pearly whites; just choose a toothbrush made from recycled materials.

Recycline (www.recycline.com) makes its toothbrush handles from recycled yogurt cups. When it's time to replace your toothbrush, mail it back to the company in a postage-paid mailer and your old toothbrush will be turned into products like outdoor furniture.

Radius uses replaceable toothbrush heads and makes handles from Nebraska maize. You can buy toothbrushes online (www. radiustoothbrush.com) or at natural foods retailers.

An alternative to this idea that works better for me is:

_____

_____

February 7

Plan your route using an online map.

The colorful paper maps sold at the gas station can be difficult (or impossible) to recycle because of the amount of ink used. Use the Internet to get directions and print an online map instead. You can use the "draft" mode on your printer to use less ink, print the map on scrap paper, and make sure it goes in the recycle box when you're finished with it. You'll get step-by-step directions to your destination and save yourself the hassle of trying to unfold and read a huge city map while you're driving—all with less waste.

Make your driving directions even greener by using the "send to phone" feature offered by websites like MapQuest and Yahoo! Maps. Turn-by-turn directions will be sent to your cell phone. You'll have paperless directions to navigate to your destination.

An alternative to this idea that works better for me is:

_____

_____

February 8

Add your fireplace ashes to the compost pile.

Let the ashes from your fireplace cool and then mix them into your compost pile. The leftover ashes are a valuable soil amendment that will help nourish your garden next spring.

An alternative to this idea that works better for me is:
_____
_____

February 9

Fill out the luggage tags that come with your suitcase, or buy plastic ones.

Most airlines provide flimsy paper tags at the check-in counter. Instead of filling out a new luggage tag—and wasting a ton of paper—every time you travel, use the tag that came with your suitcase, or buy one. You'll want to have a sturdier luggage tag attached to your suitcase in case it gets lost (there is no guarantee the paper tag is going to survive a detour and find its way back to you!).

An alternative to this idea that works better for me is:

_____

_____

February 10

Watch the tachometer in your car.

The tachometer measures how fast your engine is turning in revolutions per minute (rpm). Keeping your engine from revving above 3,000 rpm can help save gas and extend the life of your car.

An alternative to this idea that works better for me is:
_____
_____

February 11

Support a green business.

You can have an impact on the environment simply by supporting eco-friendly businesses. Have dinner at a restaurant that uses local ingredients, shop at a boutique that sells organic cotton t-shirts, or stay at a hotel that uses solar energy.

Go to www.onepercentfortheplanet.org/en to find a list of businesses that give 1 percent of their profits to environmental causes. You can buy all of the things you need, from coffee and wine to cleaning products and camping gear, from businesses that care about the planet.

An alternative to this idea that works better for me is:

_____

_____

February 12

Defrost food in the refrigerator.

You could race home after work and run a package of frozen chicken breasts under hot water to defrost them for dinner. But running the tap uses two to three gallons of water per minute. You can save a lot of water by putting chicken breasts (or any other frozen foods that need to be thawed in time for dinner) in the refrigerator first thing in the morning and let them defrost during the day.

> Thawing food in the refrigerator is also safer. According to the U.S. Department of Agriculture, foods should never be defrosted with hot water because it increases the likelihood of food-borne illnesses.

An alternative to this idea that works better for me is:

_____

_____

February 13

Order eco-friendly flowers for your Valentine.

They may be the traditional symbol of love, but red roses are not a green choice. All roses are typically sprayed with chemicals to kill insects and mildew and are dunked in preservatives to keep them from rotting before they're shipped. Ask your florist about organic roses, which are grown without pesticides or preservatives. The buds might cost a little more, but it's worth the extra money to show your love for the planet.

An alternative to this idea that works better for me is:

_____

_____

February 14

Surprise your Valentine with a candlelight dinner.

Turning out the lights isn't just romantic, it saves energy. To make the evening even more eco-friendly, opt for soy candles over candles made from paraffin. Soy candles are made from natural ingredients, last longer than paraffin candles, and reduce the amount of soot released into the air by 90 percent.

An alternative to this idea that works better for me is:
_____
_____

DONE

February 15

Trade your plastic water bottle for a stainless-steel version.

Stainless-steel water bottles look trendy, but more importantly, they are free of bisphenol A (BPA), a toxic substance used to make clear and shatterproof plastic. BPA has been linked to cancer, interferes with fertility, and could contribute to childhood behavioral problems like hyperactivity.

An alternative to this idea that works better for me is:

_____

_____

February 16

Download your favorite songs online.

It takes a lot of raw materials to manufacture a compact disc. In addition to the disc itself, each CD is packaged in a plastic jewel case. Downloading music is a much more eco-friendly alternative. Digital downloads also eliminate the need for liner notes and plastic wrapping used to seal CD cases. Go to www.apple.com/itunes or www.amazon.com to download your favorite tunes without harming the planet.

An alternative to this idea that works better for me is:

_____

_____

February 17

Cancel your newspaper subscription and read the news online instead.

The newspapers delivered to your front door every morning pile up quickly. Newspapers can (and should) be recycled, but it still takes a lot of resources to produce a paper, from the trees that are cut to manufacture the paper and the chemicals used to produce ink to the energy used to run the printing press.

Reading the news online is an eco-friendly alternative. Go to www.cnn.com for up-to-date national news and visit the websites of your local newspaper and TV stations to find out what is happening in your community.

An alternative to this idea that works better for me is:

_____

_____

February 18

If you're a beer drinker, order a beer on tap while at a bar or restaurant.

Draft beer is an environmentally friendly alternative to drinking bottled beer. Draft beer eliminates the need for glass bottles and cardboard packaging so you can enjoy your favorite brew without guilt.

An alternative to this idea that works better for me is:

February 19

Use a vinegar solution to clean the house.

Vinegar is not just for salad dressing—it's also a powerful all-purpose household cleaner! A bottle of vinegar is considerably cheaper than similar-size bottles of brand name cleaning products and much safer.

Most commercial cleaning products contain harsh chemicals that pollute the air in your home. In 2000, cleaning products were also responsible for nearly 10 percent of all toxic exposures reported to poison control centers.

> Never mix vinegar with bleach, ammonia, or products containing ammonia (like dish soap) because the fumes are toxic.

Use a mixture of equal parts vinegar and water to tackle jobs ranging from cleaning windows and cutting through soap scum to removing stains.

An alternative to this idea that works better for me is:

_____

_____

February 20

Research green dry cleaners in your neighborhood.

Most dry cleaners use a solvent called per-chloroethylene (commonly called perc) that poses serious health risks like headaches, nausea, and skin irritation. Perc is also a hazardous air pollutant. Fortunately, a growing number of dry cleaners are going green.

Some eco-friendly dry cleaners use silicone-based solvents while others use liquid carbon dioxide to clean your clothes. Both are nontoxic alternatives to perc. Go to www.greenearthcleaning.com for a list of eco-friendly dry cleaners in your area.

An alternative to this idea that works better for me is:
_____
_____

February 21

Switch on your ceiling fan.

In the winter, ceiling fans recirculate heat into the living areas and can reduce your energy bill by up to 10 percent. Some energy-efficient models use as little energy as a 100-watt light bulb.

Remember to reverse the fan motor in the winter months. Ceiling fans come with forward and reverse settings. Use the forward setting in the summer to blow cool air down into the room and the reverse setting in the winter to circulate warm air.

The U.S. Environmental Protection Agency recommends hanging the fan so that its blades are at least one foot below the ceiling, seven feet above the floor, and two feet from the nearest wall for maximum efficiency.

An alternative to this idea that works better for me is:

_____

_____

February 22

Use natural de-icer on your car.

Instead of the chemical-laden solutions designed to keep ice from building up on your car windows (or letting your car idle to warm up and melt the ice), rub the inside of the windows with a sponge soaked in salt water. You won't notice it but the salt residue will remain on the windows and will help ward off frost.

An alternative to this idea that works better for me is:

_____

_____

February 23

Keep food waste out of the garbage disposal.

The peach pits and cucumber peels that you put in the garbage disposal eventually end up in streams and lakes where they deprive the water of oxygen and kill aquatic life like algae and fish. Running the garbage disposal also uses a lot of water. Instead, add food waste to your compost pile (see July 6). No compost pile? Put food scraps in the trash. Once food reaches the landfill, it biodegrades over time.

An alternative to this idea that works better for me is:

_____

_____

February 24

Buy rechargeable batteries.

Over 15 billion batteries are used every year and most end up in the landfill. Batteries contain toxic heavy metals like nickel, mercury, and cadmium that leach into lakes and streams and pollute the air.

You can dramatically reduce the number of batteries that end up in the landfill by disposing of them properly at local recycling centers. Rechargeable batteries are an even better option. Some rechargeable batteries can be recharged up to 1,000 times, taking the place of hundreds of single-use batteries in your lifetime.

An alternative to this idea that works better for me is:
_____
_____

February 25

Sign up for paperless billing.

Ask your bank, energy provider, and credit card companies to send your monthly statements via e-mail. Paper bills account for almost 700,000 tons of waste and 2 million tons of carbon dioxide per year. Once you've paid your bills, view your bank statements online to ensure that all of the transactions were completed.

An alternative to this idea that works better for me is:

_____

_____

February 26

Turn off the water before you leave for spring break.

You can turn off the water with the main shut-off valve, which is located on the water meter. Turn the valve in a clockwise direction until it is completely turned off. When you return from vacation, turn the valve back on.

You'll prevent the faucets from dripping, the icemaker from working overtime, and the toilets from running. In the winter, it's possible for pipes to freeze and break if the water is unused for long periods of time, which increases the risk of flooding.

An alternative to this idea that works better for me is:

February 27

Choose the right burner on the stove when you're making dinner.

You can minimize the amount of energy you use to cook dinner by using the right burner for the size of the pan. If the circumference of the burner is larger than the size of the pan, you're leaking unused heat into the air. Also avoid using a pot that is too big; it takes a lot of extra energy to heat the contents.

An alternative to this idea that works better for me is:
_____
_____

February 28

Snip the plastic rings that are used to package six-packs of beer and soda.

We've all heard horror stories about plastic six-pack rings suffocating fish and getting tangled around the beaks of birds and other wildlife. Remember to snip the rings before tossing them in the trash. Better yet, eliminate them altogether by buying single sodas or cases that come in cardboard packaging.

An alternative to this idea that works better for me is:

_____

_____

March 1

Use hydrogen peroxide instead of bleach when you wash a load of whites.

Bleach is toxic to marine life and creates a by-product called dioxin which is a known carcinogen and has been linked to birth defects. Once it goes down the drain, its impact is irreversible.

Hydrogen peroxide is just as effective for whitening your clothes but has none of the harmful environmental effects of bleach. In fact, hydrogen peroxide is simply water with an extra oxygen molecule. It is produced naturally in the environment when sunlight mixes with water. Add a cup of 3 percent hydrogen peroxide to your wash as an inexpensive and color-safe alternative to bleach; your clothes will look great and you'll be doing your part to safeguard marine life.

An alternative to this idea that works better for me is:
_____
_____

March 2

Use cloth napkins at dinner.

The average American uses 2,200 two-ply paper napkins per year. Switch to cloth napkins and you'll help keep more than 662 billion paper napkins out of the trash.

Choose cloth napkins made from organic cotton, which is grown without harmful pesticides. You can be even more eco-friendly by washing your cloth napkins in cold water and hanging them to dry. If you must use paper napkins, make sure they're made from 100 percent recycled paper content.

An alternative to this idea that works better for me is:

_____

_____

March 3

Toast your commitment to the environment with a glass of organic wine.

Organic wines are made with grapes that have not been sprayed with pesticides and contain no added sulfites, acids that occur naturally in most wines but are often added as preservatives.

Start stocking your wine rack with sulfite-free organic wines and encourage your friends to do the same.

An alternative to this idea that works better for me is:

_____

_____

March 4

Make a bowl of popcorn, turn off the lights, and curl up with a documentary about the environment.

DVDs like *An Inconvenient Truth* and *The 11th Hour* highlight the severity of the environmental issues around the globe and offer solutions for change. Invite friends and family to watch with you and begin talking about how you can help protect the environment from further degradation.

An alternative to this idea that works better for me is:

_____

_____

March 5

Make a list of the items you could buy in bulk.

Buying in bulk helps keep excess packaging from the landfills and cuts down on the number of trips you make to the supermarket.

Everything from pasta and dog food to toilet tissue and motor oil is sold in bulk. The key is finding bulk items that contain larger quantities of the product without excess packaging. Stay away from products that are bundled together in a cardboard box and covered in plastic.

An alternative to this idea that works better for me is:

_____

_____

March 6

Recycle!

You can have a huge impact on the environment by recycling. If everyone in the United States took a few minutes a week to separate their plastic, paper, and aluminum products from the regular trash, the amount of waste sent to the landfills would be reduced by 75 percent. Remember, recycling is the law in some states. You can increase your odds of recycling by putting a recycling box in every room in the house.

The current recycling rate in the United States is just 33 percent. Do your part to boost the recycling rate by reminding your co-worker to put her soda can in the office recycling bin and encouraging your friends to buy products with recycled packaging.

An alternative to this idea that works better for me is:

_____

_____

March 7

Research eco-friendly cruises for your upcoming vacation.

Cruise lines are working hard to minimize their environmental impact by implementing towel reuse programs, participating in onboard recycling, and maximizing their energy efficiency. Some cruise lines are even offering carbon-neutral cruises. The promise: enough trees will be planted to absorb the greenhouse gas emissions from a cruise.

While you're on board, ask the environmental officer (all ships have at least one on every cruise) how you can further minimize the environmental impact of your vacation.

An alternative to this idea that works better for me is:
_____
_____

March 8

Snap pictures with a digital camera.

It takes a lot of resources to manufacture film, and processing the 686 million rolls of film that are developed every year requires harsh chemicals. A digital camera allows you to print your favorite images and store the rest electronically, cutting down on waste. Most digital cameras also use rechargeable batteries, making them even more eco-friendly.

An alternative to this idea that works better for me is:

_____

_____

DONE ○

March 9

Recycle your telephone books.

Currently, telephone books account for 10 percent of all the waste in the landfills. There is an even more eco-friendly option: call your local phone company and ask to stop phonebook delivery. You can look up phone numbers online instead.

An alternative to this idea that works better for me is:

_____

_____

March 10

Drink filtered water instead of bottled water.

More than 38 billion water bottles end up in landfills every year where they take an average of 700 years before they even begin to decompose. It takes over 1.5 million barrels of oil—enough to fuel 10,000 cars—to manufacture the number of plastic water bottles that Americans drink from on an annual basis. Switching to tap water will conserve valuable resources and significantly reduce waste.

An alternative to this idea that works better for me is:

_____

_____

March 11

Upgrade your phone service to include voicemail.

Answering machines need to be plugged in around the clock and can use up to 100 kWh of energy per year—the same amount of energy required to wash 30 loads of laundry in hot water. If all of the answering machines in the United States were replaced with voicemail systems, the emissions savings would be equivalent to taking 250,000 cars off the road.

Remember to recycle your old answering machine. Like other electronic devices, answering machines need to be disposed of properly. Call your local waste-management facility to find out how to recycle your answering machine.

An alternative to this idea that works better for me is:

March 12

Ask your barista for a cup of eco-friendly coffee.

Coffees labeled "organic" and "shade grown" help prevent soil erosion, reduce pollution, and preserve wildlife habitats and rainforest ecosystems. You can have even more of an impact by choosing coffee that is Fair Trade certified: it ensures that coffee growers are getting a fair price for their crops.

> Every U.S. household that switches to eco-friendly coffee helps protect more than 9,000 square feet of rainforest. Check supermarket shelves for organic and shade-grown blends to brew at home.

An alternative to this idea that works better for me is:

_____

_____

March 13

Shop for a great outfit at a secondhand store or vintage boutique instead of hitting the mall.

Americans dispose of more than 4 billion tons of clothing every year. Fabrics can take hundreds of years to break down in the landfill. Vintage clothes aren't just fashionable; shopping second-hand means you'll get a one-of-a-kind look and help keep clothes out of the landfill.

An alternative to this idea that works better for me is:

_____

_____

March 14

Don't top off your gas tank.

It's tempting to fill your gas tank just a little more after hearing the clicking of the auto shutoff valve on the gas pump. Resist the urge. You need to leave some extra room in your gas tank to allow the gasoline to expand. Topping off the tank may cause gas to evaporate into the vapor collection system in your car, causing the vehicle to run poorly and increase its emissions. You also increase the odds of gas spilling and causing excess air pollution when you attempt to top off the tank.

An alternative to this idea that works better for me is:

_____

_____

March 15

Donate your used athletic shoes.

The rubber soles of athletic shoes can be recycled and turned into surface material for basketball courts, athletic fields, running tracks, and playgrounds all over the country.

The Nike Reuse-a-Shoe program is the largest shoe recycling program in the United States and has recycled approximately 20 million pairs of running shoes. Go to www.letmeplay.com/reuseashoe to find out where to drop off your used sneakers.

An alternative to this idea that works better for me is:
_____
_____

March 16

Buy your dog a leash made of canvas or hemp.

Most dog leashes are made of nylon. Nitrous oxide, a greenhouse gas associated with global warming, is emitted during the production of nylon.

Replacing all of the nylon pet leashes in the United States would prevent the release of the same amount of greenhouse gasses produced by 250,000 households per year.

An alternative to this idea that works better for me is:
_____
_____

March 17

Research options for eco-friendly furniture.

Whether it's time to replace your old coffee table or buy a crib for your new addition, it's important to know what you're buying. Furniture made from plywood, laminated wood, and particle board contains high levels of formaldehyde, a chemical that causes headaches, respiratory irritation, and skin rashes. It's also a known carcinogen. Instead, look for furniture made from low-VOC paint and finishes or buy unfinished hardwood furniture and coat it yourself with water-based polyurethane sealer.

An alternative to this idea that works better for me is:

_____

_____

March 18

Change the margins on your Word documents.

The default margins on the documents you print are 1.25 inches on all sides. Simply changing the margins to .75 inches will reduce the amount of paper you use by almost 5 percent. It might not seem like a lot, but if everyone in the United States made the change, we would save $400 million and a forest the size of Rhode Island!

Changing your margins is simple. If you have a PC, open a Word document, select File and then Page Setup. Click on the Margins tab and type in .75 inches. You'll be asked, "Do you want to change the default settings for the page setup?" Click Yes, and all the documents you print in the future will have smaller margins.

If you have a Macintosh, open Word, go to Format, and then Document. Click on Margins and change the settings.

An alternative to this idea that works better for me is:

_____

_____

March 19

Buy a razor with replaceable blades.

Disposable razors account for close to 2 million pounds of virgin plastics that are dumped in the landfill every year. The plastic handles are not biodegradable or recyclable. Disposable razors also contain much more packaging than a single razor and packages of replaceable blades.

An alternative to this idea that works better for me is:

_____

_____

March 20

Store your files electronically.

Americans use over 90 million tons of paper—almost 700 pounds per person—per year. You can cut down on the amount of paper you use by storing your files electronically instead of printing important documents and storing them in a filing cabinet. Create folders on your computer to make it easy to find important documents with the click of a mouse.

An alternative to this idea that works better for me is:

_____

_____

March 21

Wash your hair with a two-in-one shampoo and conditioner.

Switching to a two-in-one product will save you time (and water) in the shower. Cutting your daily shower by 2 minutes will save 1,825 gallons of water per year—that's a whopping 7,300 gallons of water for a family of four! You'll also reduce waste by 50 percent because there is only one bottle to recycle.

An alternative to this idea that works better for me is:

March 22

Say no to ATM receipts.

The receipts from 8 billion ATM transactions per year are one of the biggest sources of litter on the planet. If Americans declined their ATM receipts, it would save a roll of paper more than 2 billion feet long—enough paper to circle the equator more than 15 times!

Tracking your account activity online means you don't need paper receipts—all of your transaction records can be viewed on your computer.

You can also cut down on paper waste (and trips to the bank) by having your paycheck automatically deposited into your bank account.

An alternative to this idea that works better for me is:

March 23

Skip the towel service at the gym.

If just 1 percent of fitness club members stopped using the towels provided at the gym and instead brought their own, it would save 4,000 loads of laundry—the equivalent of 36 million gallons of water a day!

Conserve additional resources by using your towel more than once, washing it in cold water with phosphate-free detergent (see April 17) and hanging it to dry.

An alternative to this idea that works better for me is:

_____

_____

March 24

Sign up for a membership to rent your favorite accessories.

You could go out and buy a trendy handbag, or you could rent it instead. Bag Borrow or Steal (www.bagborrowsteal.com) charges a monthly fee to let members rent handbags by designers like Gucci, Prada, and Louis Vuitton. You can use a handbag for a special evening out or take your favorite on a monthlong vacation. Once you're done with it, simply return it and request a new bag. The program helps cut down on the raw materials and energy used to make new handbags.

An alternative to this idea that works better for me is:
_____
_____

March 25

Share your feelings about going green.

You can talk about your experiences and read what others have to say about their eco-friendly lifestyle at www.truegreenconfessions.com. The site invites users to post comments ranging from "I have become addicted to composting" to "I hate that my boyfriend doesn't recycle." It's a great place to ask for advice and learn what others are doing to live green.

An alternative to this idea that works better for me is:

_____

_____

March 26

Put your dryer lint in the backyard.

The soft lint is ideal for birds to feather their nests and is a much more eco-friendly alternative than throwing it in the garbage. Simply place the dryer lint in a pile on the ground and wait for nesting birds to retrieve it.

An alternative to this idea that works better for me is:

_____

_____

March 27

Close your curtains!

Keeping your curtains closed during the winter will help prevent heat from escaping and keep the cold air from seeping into the house. Make sure your curtains are not blocking heat registers, which can force your furnace to work harder.

An alternative to this idea that works better for me is:

_____

_____

March 28

Hang a bird feeder and keep it well-stocked with birdseed.

Birds will flock to your yard, giving you a glimpse of the natural world. More than 50 million Americans have bird feeders in their yards, and the extra food can help birds survive in extreme temperatures and heavy snow.

Dirty bird feeders spread salmonella and avian pox, and moldy birdseed can transmit fungal infections. Be sure to clean your bird feeder at least twice a year using mild liquid dish detergent and warm water.

An alternative to this idea that works better for me is:
_____
_____

DONE

March 29

Research eco-friendly paint for your next home improvement project.

Environmentally friendly paints meet federal standards for low levels of volatile organic compounds (VOCs), which release harmful pollutants into the air. Low-VOC paints are available in hundreds of different colors, and they are also low odor so there is no lingering new-paint smell. Unlike other green products (think organic produce) that tend to be more expensive, eco-friendly paint costs about the same as regular paint.

Eco-friendly paint is available at home improvement centers and paint retailers nationwide.

An alternative to this idea that works better for me is:
_____
_____

March 30

Change the setting on your printer.

It's estimated that 240 million printer cartridges end up in landfills every year. You can extend the life of your printer cartridge by printing unimportant documents in draft mode, which uses less ink. Read your owner's manual for your printer to find out how to print your documents in draft mode.

> In the United States, nearly one million empty ink cartridges are thrown away every day. Stores like OfficeMax and Office Depot allow you to refill your ink cartridges instead of buying new ones.

When the time comes to replace your printer cartridge, be sure to recycle the old one. Better yet, choose printer cartridges that are refillable to help reduce waste.

An alternative to this idea that works better for me is:
_____
_____

March 31

Store your winter clothes without mothballs.

Mothballs might keep moths from nibbling holes in your favorite sweater, but their toxins are harmful to the environment. Mothballs are made from dichlorobenzene, a pesticide that gets into the groundwater and can be toxic to animals.

There are more environmentally friendly options for storing your winter clothes: put them in an airtight container with bay leaves or cedar blocks—both are natural materials that will repel moths and keep your clothes smelling fresh until next year.

An alternative to this idea that works better for me is:

_____

_____

April 1

Look for the recycling label on the packaging of the products in your home.

Containers that can be recycled contain the familiar symbol along with a number. Every recycling company has different regulations for what can be recycled in your area. Some companies accept all plastics while others can only recycle plastics with lower numbers. Call your local waste-management company or visit their website to find out which products can be recycled in your area.

An alternative to this idea that works better for me is:

_____

_____

April 2

Calculate the impact your paper choices have on the environment.

The Environmental Defense Fund has a paper calculator that allows you to enter details about your current paper use to learn how to make more environmentally friendly choices. Choosing the right paper can cut pollution and save valuable resources like wood and water. Visit www.edf.org/papercalculator to start calculating.

An alternative to this idea that works better for me is:

_____

_____

April 3

Share your favorite magazines.

Every ton of paper you help divert from the landfill helps save 1.2 tons of greenhouse gas emissions from going into the atmosphere. So once you're finished reading about your favorite celebrities and home decorating trends, donate your magazines to a local hospital or nursing home or drop them off at the gym.

An alternative to this idea that works better for me is:
_____
_____

April 4

When it comes time to dye Easter eggs, go green. You can use ingredients from your kitchen cupboard to create brightly colored Easter eggs, naturally.

Most of the egg-dyeing kits sold in craft stores and supermarkets are made from coal tar and other petroleum-based products. Certain food dyes have been linked to health problems such as allergies, chromosomal damage, and cancer.

Make bright yellow dye by mixing two teaspoons of ground turmeric powder with ⅔ cup of boiling water and one teaspoon of white vinegar. Let the mixture cool and start dyeing your Easter eggs.

> Make your egg-decorating party even more eco-friendly by using organic, free-range eggs and composting leftover materials when you're done.

One cup of frozen grape juice from concentrate mixed with one teaspoon of vinegar will create beautiful purple dye. Let the mixture sit overnight before dyeing the eggs.

Red dye can be created using four tablespoons of freshly grated beets, ⅔ cup of boiling water, and one teaspoon of white vinegar. Mix the ingredients together and begin decorating.

An alternative to this idea that works better for me is:

_____

_____

April 5

Use a reel mower to cut your lawn.

Every weekend, 54 million Americans cut their grass, using more than 800 million gallons of gasoline annually. Switching from a gas-powered lawn mower to a reel mower will keep 80 pounds of CO_2 out of the air every year per mower. Reel mowers also reduce neighborhood noise pollution.

An alternative to this idea that works better for me is:

_____

_____

April 6

Buy solar lights for your home or garden.

Solar lights are charged by the sun. Once the sun goes down, the self-charging lights cast a soft glow along garden paths and light up the patio—without using the energy required to power electric lighting.

An alternative to this idea that works better for me is:
_____
_____

April 7

Learn more about xeriscaping.

Xeriscaping is the latest trend in eco-friendly gardening. It involves choosing drought-tolerant plants such as sedum and thyme that will thrive with very little water. Xeriscaping can reduce landscape water use by at least 60 percent. Learn more about xeriscaping at sites such as www.coloradowaterwise.org, and plan on incorporating some of the principles into your garden this spring.

An alternative to this idea that works better for me is:

_____

_____

April 8

Cut back on the number of documents you're printing.

The average American uses 700 pounds of paper per year. Making a few small changes can significantly reduce the amount of paper that ends up in your recycling bin. Print documents only when you must have a hard copy, and print on both sides of the paper. Keep a stack of scrap paper on hand for printing drafts and personal documents.

Choosing paper made from recycled content will also help decrease your environmental impact.

Also, changing the setting on your printer can help extend the life of your printer cartridge (see March 30).

An alternative to this idea that works better for me is:

April 9

Switch to eco-friendly diapers.

Disposable diapers are made from plastic and absorptive acrylic gels that are not biodegradable. They are also bleached, and the harsh chemicals used in the bleaching process can be a skin irritant and releases carcinogenic and endocrine-disrupting toxins. Retailers like Gaiam and Whole Foods Markets sell chlorine-free diapers that are gentler on your baby's skin and kinder to the environment.

An alternative to this idea that works better for me is:
_____
_____

April 10

Research your next big purchase to learn more about its environmental impact.

Consumer Reports has launched a website to rate items ranging from towels and water filters to refrigerators and cars. In addition to rating their overall performance, special attention is paid to the eco-friendliness of the products. Go to www.greenerchoices.org before making your next big purchase.

An alternative to this idea that works better for me is:

_____

_____

April 11

Dispose of old paint.

It's almost impossible to judge how much paint you'll need to complete a project, so you often wind up with half-empty buckets in your basement or attic.

Most paints contain toxic solvents and heavy metals, so the leftovers cannot be tossed in the trash.

To dispose of water-based paint, fill a plastic-lined box with cat litter or sawdust, pour the paint into the container, and let it dry before putting it in the garbage. Oil-based paints need to be taken to community recycling depots where experts will dispose of it properly.

> Never pour paint down the drain; it will clog the pipes and pollute the water supply.

An alternative to this idea that works better for me is:

_____

_____

April 12

Donate to a nonprofit organization.

It's tax time! Do the environment a favor and make a donation to a nonprofit organization that supports environmental causes. Donate to the Audubon Society if you want to help protect endangered birds, or support the World Wildlife Fund if you're concerned about global warming. Make sure to keep a receipt of your donation for tax purposes.

The American Institute of Philanthropy (www.charitywatch. org) rates national charities and offers tips for giving wisely. Before you write a check, ask the organization how it's going to spend your money. A reputable charity will be happy to explain how it uses the donations it receives and will provide annual reports and financial statements at your request.

An alternative to this idea that works better for me is:

April 13

Take a hike!

Going on a spring hike is a great way to experience nature. Ensure that your hike has as little impact on the environment as possible by following "leave no trace" principles: take nothing but photographs, leave nothing but footprints.

You can make your hike even more eco-friendly by returning trail maps to their post at the trailhead instead of tossing them in the trash.

An alternative to this idea that works better for me is:

_____

_____

April 14

File your taxes electronically.

You can't avoid filing your taxes, but you can avoid using reams of paper to send your documents to Uncle Sam. Every year, more than 72 million tax returns are filed electronically. It would save 660 million sheets of paper if every tax return in the United States were filed electronically.

An alternative to this idea that works better for me is:

_____

_____

April 15

Request an electronic tax refund.

You could let the IRS mail you a check or you can have your refund deposited directly into your account. Every year, the IRS has to print and mail 54 million tax refunds to individual taxpayers across the United States.

An alternative to this idea that works better for me is:
_____
_____

April 16

Unclog a plugged drain with an eco-friendly solution of baking soda and vinegar.

Chemical cleaners might be successful at unclogging your sink, but they are highly toxic. The ingredients are corrosive and the vapors are noxious. Pouring chemical cleaners down the drain also pollutes the water supply.

Mix ½ cup of baking soda with ½ cup of white vinegar. The fizzy mixture will remove most of the buildup clogging your drainpipe. Eliminate the unpleasant smell of the mixture by pouring lemon juice down the drain once the clog is removed.

An alternative to this idea that works better for me is:

_____

_____

April 17

Buy phosphate-free laundry detergent.

Conventional laundry detergents often contain phosphates, one of the biggest causes of ocean pollution. Phosphates can cause algae blooms, which kill marine life by depleting the water of oxygen.

Although they have been banned in many areas, many cleaning products like laundry detergent are still made with phosphates. Shop for detergents that are phosphate-free and follow the directions on the container to avoid overuse.

An alternative to this idea that works better for me is:
_____
_____

April 18

Spice up your meals with fresh herbs.

Instead of buying heavily packaged herbs at the grocery store (which often travel thousands of miles before reaching supermarket shelves), try growing your own at home. It's easy to grow common herbs like rosemary, thyme, and oregano indoors. All you need are a few supplies and a bit of patience.

Buy your favorite herbs from a local garden center, plant them in small containers filled with potting soil, and water them thoroughly. Choose a location that gets at least five hours of sunlight per day and keep the soil damp.

Use your indoor herb garden to cut a bit of oregano the next time you're making spaghetti sauce or add a sprig of mint to your favorite drink. Enjoy the scent of fresh herbs that fills the house.

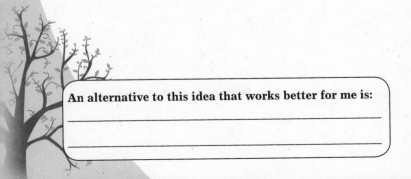

An alternative to this idea that works better for me is:

_____

_____

April 19

Donate old newspapers to your local animal shelter.

Animal rescue organizations use newspaper as bedding for pets awaiting adoption. Call your local humane society to find out if they're in need of used newspapers. Ask about donating old, clean towels, too. Many rescue organizations also post wish lists on their websites.

An alternative to this idea that works better for me is:

_____

_____

April 20

Return wire hangers to the dry cleaner to be recycled.

Every year, 3.5 billion wire hangers end up in the landfill. Your dry cleaner will reuse wire hangers for the next customer. Most dry cleaners will even accept wire hangers in poor condition. Instead of being reused, they'll likely be sent to a scrap metal dealer or returned to the supplier.

An alternative to this idea that works better for me is:

_____

_____

April 21

Set the cruise control in your car.

You can improve your fuel efficiency by using cruise control on the highway. Cruise control will help you maintain a steady speed, resulting in fuel savings of up to 10 percent.

An alternative to this idea that works better for me is:
_____
_____

April 22

Celebrate Earth Day by planting a tree.

The cooling effect of a young tree is equivalent to that of 10 air conditioners operating 20 hours a day. Planting a tree can significantly decrease your energy bills.

Choose a tree from your local nursery and plant it properly in order to ensure its survival.

Bare root seedlings: Keeping the roots moist, dig a hole as deep as the longest root and twice as wide as the root cluster. Build a small mound of soil at the base of the hole, place the roots on the mound, and fill the hole. Water it generously.

Burlapped roots: Dig a hole that is twice as wide and just as deep as the root ball. Place the tree in the middle of the hole, remove the burlap, fill the hole with soil, and water it well.

Potted trees: Dig a hole that is twice as wide and just as deep as the container. Gently remove the container and shake the roots loose from the soil. Place the tree in the hole, fill with soil, and water generously.

An alternative to this idea that works better for me is:

_____

_____

April 23

Clean the kitchen with a cloth dishrag instead of paper towels.

If every family in the U.S. replaced one 70-sheet roll of paper towels with a reusable alternative, it could save 544,000 trees. That adds up to 6,528,000 trees per year for families who use one roll of paper towels per month. If you must use paper towels, choose brands that are made from recycled content.

An alternative to this idea that works better for me is:

DONE

April 24

Take your own mug to the coffee shop.

Americans use 16 billion paper cups per year. You can help reduce that number by asking your barista to fill a reusable mug. Stainless-steel travel mugs are long lasting and will keep your coffee hot. Best of all, many coffee shops will give you a discount for bringing your own mug.

An alternative to this idea that works better for me is:

_____

_____

April 25

Shop for eco-friendly beauty products.

Parabens, toxins that have been linked to breast cancer, are found in everything from shampoos and shaving gels to lipstick and moisturizer. Ingredients like coal tar (used in shampoos) and phthalates (used in nail polish and perfumes) have also been linked to cancer and fertility problems.

Using natural alternatives like almond and coconut oil for moisturizers and other paraben-free beauty products helps keep toxic chemicals out of your bloodstream and out of the water supply. Shop for personal-care items with the USDA Organic seal, which indicates the product has been certified at least 95 percent organic.

An alternative to this idea that works better for me is:
_____
_____

April 26

Set up a worm compost bin.

Worms eat food scraps, which become compost after digestion. You can create a worm bin by following the easy steps below.

Choose a container (plastic or glass works best) that is no more than 12 inches deep and has a lid. Line the bottom with strips of moistened newspaper or leaves. Fill the bin with red worms or red wigglers from a garden center (you'll need approximately two pounds of worms for every one pound of food waste you generate per day). Put the worms and food waste into the bin. Avoid meat, oil, and dairy products, which are more difficult for the worms to compost and can attract pests.

After three to five months, your worm bin will fill with compost. Prepare to harvest the compost by not adding new food scraps to the bin for at least two weeks. Push the contents to once side of the worm bin and add fresh bedding and food scraps to the other side. The worms will move to the fresh side of the bin, leaving their compost behind. Remove the compost and use it in your garden.

An alternative to this idea that works better for me is:

_____

_____

April 27

Join a community-supported agriculture (CSA) program.

Local farms often sell "shares" in their farm; you'll pay a small fee at the beginning of the growing season, and in return you'll receive a box of fresh produce—delivered to your door—every week.

CSAs encourage stewardship of the land and promote the preservation of small farms. They also ensure that farmers are getting a fair price for their produce and help members learn about the origins of their food. Produce delivered through a CSA is not transported long distances, cutting down on greenhouse-gas emissions. Find a CSA in your community at www.localharvest.org.

An alternative to this idea that works better for me is:

April 28

Plan your vegetable garden.

Rotating the crops in your vegetable garden can help control pests. Believe it or not, planting carrots and lettuce in a different section of the garden every spring can make it more difficult for pests to find them year after year. Simple crop rotation can significantly cut down on pesticide use, which prevents chemicals from leaching into the soil and groundwater.

An alternative to this idea that works better for me is:

April 29

Reset the blade on your lawnmower.

Setting the lawnmower blade at three inches helps the grass absorb more sun and moisture. Longer grass is better at pushing out weeds, eliminating the need to apply chemical weed killers. Cutting the grass higher also means the grass clippings are shorter and will decompose (and fertilize the lawn) more quickly.

An alternative to this idea that works better for me is:
_____
_____

April 30

Feed your lawn and garden with organic fertilizer.

Chemical fertilizers have a negative impact on the environment. They can burn plants, cause the progressive decline of soil health, and lead to chemicals like nitrogen and phosphorus getting into the groundwater.

Organic fertilizers are formulated to retain soil moisture and release nutrients at a slower pace, fertilizing for longer periods with less waste. Your local garden center carries natural fertilizers like manure, worm casings, and peat as well as manufactured organic fertilizers like compost, blood meal, and bone meal. No matter which type of organic fertilizer you choose, be sure to follow the application instructions on the fertilizer bag.

An alternative to this idea that works better for me is:
_____
_____

May 1

Water your plants first thing in the morning or late in the evening.

Soil retains moisture better when the temperatures are cooler so you'll use less water if you avoid watering them in the heat of the day.

An alternative to this idea that works better for me is:
_____
_____

May 2

Install a drip irrigation system.

Drip irrigation systems apply water slowly and directly to the roots of the plant, using up to 50 percent less water than a traditional sprinkler. You can buy simple drip hoses at home improvement stores for under $30. Choose a lawn sprinkler that has an automatic shutoff device and a moisture sensor to ensure you're only watering when the lawn really needs it.

An alternative to this idea that works better for me is:

_____

_____

May 3

Visit the garden center to research drought-tolerant plants.

Landscaping with plants that require little irrigation will help you cut back on the amount of water you use in the garden. The types of plants that are drought-tolerant vary from region to region, so it's best to go to your local garden center and ask which plants will thrive without a lot of water. You'll be surprised at how many choices are available.

An alternative to this idea that works better for me is:

_____

_____

May 4

Pay attention to how much water your plants are getting.

The plants in your garden all have different watering needs; make sure that you're not giving too much water to plants that thrive in dryer soil. Overwatering wastes resources and can cause problems ranging from fungus to rotting roots. As a general rule, new plants need a lot more water than mature plants. Ask the experts at your local nursery or read the tags that came with your new plants to see how much water they need.

An alternative to this idea that works better for me is:

_____

_____

May 5

Use beer to keep slugs out of your garden.

Beer is a surefire way to keep slugs from munching on your favorite plants. Best of all, it won't harm your plants or other garden critters.

Pour an inch of beer into a small bowl and place it in the garden, level with the soil. Slugs will make their way to the edge and fall in. Add the dead slugs to your compost pile and refill the bowl.

An alternative to this idea that works better for me is:
_____

_____

May 6

Make a solution to keep dogs from digging in your garden.

A mixture of Tabasco sauce, garlic, onion, and cayenne pepper in a bucket of water will deter dogs. Let it sit for several hours and then sprinkle it over the areas of the garden where dogs have been digging.

An alternative to this idea that works better for me is:

_____

_____

May 7

Request e-tickets for your next trip.

Paper tickets are usually printed on heavy paper with colored ink. E-tickets can be printed in black and white on recycled paper. You can reduce the amount of ink used to print your e-ticket by selecting the draft mode on your printer (see March 30). At the airport, all you need is your e-ticket and a piece of identification. You can make your trip even more eco-friendly by printing your boarding pass at home.

An alternative to this idea that works better for me is:

_____

_____

May 8

Check your car tires for wear and tear.

If your tires need to be replaced, consider buying retreads instead of new tires. Retread tires are high-quality tires that meet the same safety and performance standards as new tires but use just one third of the petroleum resources to produce.

In North America, the use of retread tires saves 400 million gallons of oil every year. Retread tires also extend the life of a tire, preventing millions of tires from going to the landfill. As a bonus, retread tires also cost 30 to 50 percent less than brand-new tires.

An alternative to this idea that works better for me is:

May 9

Run outside instead of getting on the treadmill.

A 30-minute workout on the treadmill uses approximately .75 kWh of energy per day. Run outside twice a week instead, and over the course of a month, you'll conserve the amount of energy required to watch television for 12 hours or do 24 loads of laundry.

An alternative to this idea that works better for me is:
_____
_____

May 10

Toss lemon peels in the garden to keep cats from using your soil as a litter box.

Citrus scents make cats cower and sneeze, so toss a few lemon or orange peels in the garden and your cat problem will be solved. The peels are not harmful to other plants in the garden and are completely biodegradable so you can put them in the garden and forget about them.

Aphids are also repelled by citrus. Mix the grated rind from a lemon with water and spray it on any plants that are being attacked by the little bugs.

You can keep your garden from turning into a litter box for the neighborhood cats with a little bit of vinegar. Unlike the chemical cat-deterrents on the market, vinegar is a natural solution that will not harm animals. Spray undiluted white vinegar at the base of trees and plants to keep cats away. Avoid spraying the foliage and using the vinegar on young plants; the acid could burn the leaves.

An alternative to this idea that works better for me is:

May 11

Buy real terra cotta pots for your patio.

Filling your patio with lightweight plastic pots is an inexpensive way to show off colorful spring blooms. The pots might look good but they're harmful to the environment. Plastic pots are made from polyvinyl chloride (PVC), a material that is referred to as "the poison plastic."

Toxins like mercury and phthalates are released during the production of PVC and have been linked to health problems in the immune and reproductive systems. PVC is not biodegradable and cannot be recycled. In fact, tossing one PVC pot into the recycling bin can contaminate a load of 100,000 plastic bottles.

Terra cotta is a much more eco-friendly option for your garden because it's a natural material that can be recycled.

An alternative to this idea that works better for me is:

May 12

Spread cocoa shell mulch around your plants.

Unlike bark mulch, which can attract fungus and is not always made from recycled materials, cocoa shell mulch is made from the clean husks removed from roasted cacao beans used to make chocolate.

Your garden will have the sweet aroma of chocolate, but there are other benefits to using cocoa shell mulch. The texture is a natural deterrent to slugs and snails and helps prevent weeds from germinating.

It's not a good idea to use cocoa shell mulch if you have a dog. Like other chocolate products, cocoa shell mulch contains theobromine, a naturally occurring stimulant in the cocoa bean that can be toxic to animals.

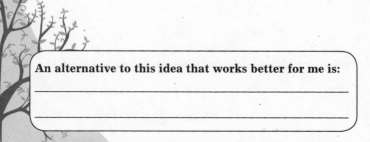

An alternative to this idea that works better for me is:

_____

_____

May 13

Research socially conscious investments.

Socially conscious investing is growing by leaps and bounds as more investors realize the benefits of putting their money into funds that operate ethically, provide social benefits, and are sensitive to the environment. Socially conscious investments account for $2.2 trillion in assets—one of every $10 invested. Learn more about socially conscious investments at www.socialinvest.org.

An alternative to this idea that works better for me is:

May 14

Neutralize carpet odors with baking soda.

Unlike specialty carpet deodorizers, which contain perfumes that can be respiratory irritants, baking powder is all-natural. Lightly dust the carpet with baking powder, let it sit for at least 20 minutes, and then vacuum. It's an inexpensive, chemical-free way to keep your home smelling fresh.

An alternative to this idea that works better for me is:

_____

_____

May 15

Pour leftover cooking grease in an aluminum can instead of down the drain.

After it cools, the liquid grease that is poured down the drain will turn into a solid and can stick to the inside of your pipes. Over time, the buildup will restrict the flow of water and may cause raw sewage to back up into your home or to overflow into streets and streams. In some cities, cooking grease that has been poured down the drain is clogging municipal sewers. Instead, pour the grease into a can and store it in the freezer. When the can is full, throw it in the garbage.

An alternative to this idea that works better for me is:

_____

_____

May 16

Donate your spare change to charity.

The coins collecting under your sofa cushions and in the ashtray of your car can make a big difference to a nonprofit organization. Collect your spare change and take it to a Coinstar machine (go to www.coinstar.com to find a machine near you) and opt to donate it to charity.

Consumers have donated more than $20 million to nonprofit organizations like the World Wildlife Fund since Coinstar started its Coins that Count program in 1997.

An alternative to this idea that works better for me is:

_____

_____

May 17

Buy a new houseplant.

You can improve the indoor air quality in your home with a few live plants. Houseplants absorb carbon dioxide while releasing oxygen into the air. In the process, they help suppress airborne mold spores and bacteria, and remove cigarette smoke as well as noxious odors from chemical-laden household cleaners. English ivy, bamboo, and spider plants are among the most effective houseplants for improving indoor air quality. Aim to have one houseplant for every 100 square feet in your home.

Some common houseplants are toxic to pets. Before you buy a houseplant, go to www. earthclinic.com/Pets/poisonous_plants.html for a comprehensive list of plants that could be harmful to your pets.

An alternative to this idea that works better for me is:

_____

_____

May 18

Park your car in the shade.

Gas evaporates from your fuel tank more quickly when you park in the sun. Parking in the shade lowers the temperature in your gas tank by up to seven degrees, significantly reducing fuel evaporation. When there is no shade available, park with your gas tank (the actual tank under the car, not the valve to fill it) facing away from the sun.

There is another benefit to parking in the shade: it keeps the temperature inside the car a little lower so you'll need less air conditioning when you get ready to drive off.

An alternative to this idea that works better for me is:
_____
_____

May 19

Make an appointment with your mechanic to have your car's air filter changed (or change it yourself).

A clogged air filter forces your car to work harder and burn more fuel. Your air filter should be changed at least once a year. Talk to your mechanic about your driving habits; your air filter might need to be replaced more often if you drive long distances or put a lot of miles on your car. A new air filter should cost less than $20 and will improve your mileage by up to 10 percent.

An alternative to this idea that works better for me is:
_____
_____

May 20

Ask your mechanic about switching to synthetic motor oil.

Conventional motor oils are derived from petroleum and need to be changed every 3,000 miles. Synthetic motor oil lasts eight times longer, which means there is less oil to dispose of. It also improves engine performance and gives you better gas mileage.

An alternative to this idea that works better for me is:

_____

_____

May 21

Shop online for clothes made from eco-friendly materials.

It takes approximately one third of a pound of chemicals to grow enough cotton for a single t-shirt. Many of those chemicals are known carcinogens that end up in streams and rivers and are harmful to wildlife.

Clothes made from organic cotton, soy, and bamboo are fashionable and will not harm the planet. Retailers such as Nike, Patagonia, and American Apparel have huge selections of clothing made from eco-friendly fibers that let you wear your beliefs on your sleeve—literally.

An alternative to this idea that works better for me is:
_____
_____

May 22

Go out for an ice cream cone.

Your favorite summertime treat is much more eco-friendly if you order it in a cone instead of a cup. A plastic spoon and dish need to be tossed in the trash, but you can consume the entire ice cream cone. The average American consumes 5.5 gallons of ice cream per year—that adds up to a lot of waste if you're eating it out of a plastic dish.

An alternative to this idea that works better for me is:

_____

_____

May 23

Fill your gas tank at night.

In the summer, hot air increases the concentration of fumes escaping from the gas pumps. Pumping gas at night (or when the temperatures are cooler) will reduce the ozone-depleting fumes released into the air.

> Be on the lookout for gas stations that have fume-capturing devices on their pumps. The rubberized caps help capture the fumes while you're pumping gas.

An alternative to this idea that works better for me is:

_____

_____

May 24

Check movie listings—and print your tickets—online.

Printing movie tickets from your personal computer allows you to use black and white ink and print in draft mode (see March 30). The plain copy paper in your printer is also easier to recycle than the paperboard used to print tickets at the theater.

An alternative to this idea that works better for me is:

_____

_____

May 25

Download software upgrades online.

Most computer software is packaged in cardboard boxes that are sealed in plastic, and the CDs are not recyclable. Software sales have tripled in the past decade, reaching $9.5 billion in 2007; downloading programs online will significantly cut back on waste.

An alternative to this idea that works better for me is:
_____
_____

May 26

Plant mint to keep mice from invading your garden.

Traps and bait can harm beneficial wildlife as well as children and pets. Instead, plant a patch of mint around the perimeter of your garden. Mint is a natural solution to keeping mice at bay. Best of all, you can pluck sprigs of the sweet-smelling herb and add them to your favorite summer beverage.

An alternative to this idea that works better for me is:
_____
_____

May 27

Return unused or expired prescription medications to your pharmacy.

It might be tempting to flush unused medication down the toilet, but a lot of prescription meds have high concentrations of metals and other substances that are harmful to the environment and wildlife. The U.S. Fish and Wildlife Service has expressed concern that prescription medications that are flushed down the toilet are entering lakes and streams and causing deformities in the fish and waterfowl. Return unused or expired prescriptions to your pharmacy where they will be disposed of properly.

An alternative to this idea that works better for me is:

_____

_____

May 28

Shop for environmentally friendly outdoor furniture.

A lot of the outdoor furniture on the market is made from PVC, a material that has a negative impact on the environment and your health.

Opt for a patio set that is made from a green material. Plastic lumber is made from recycled plastic like yogurt containers and looks like wood. It's durable, fade-resistant, and available in a variety of colors. Wood/plastic furniture is made from recycled plastic and wood fiber. It has a more natural appearance than plastic lumber and is also highly durable. If you really want wood furniture, choose products certified by the Forest Stewardship Council (the wood will be stamped "FSC Certified") to ensure that it was harvested responsibly.

An alternative to this idea that works better for me is:

_____

_____

May 29

Donate your frequent-flier miles to a charity that is working to help the environment.

Nonprofit organizations use frequent-flier miles to support their mission, whether it's sending a terminally ill child to Disneyland or sending relief workers to help after a natural disaster. Check with your favorite nonprofit organization to see if they accept donations of frequent-flier miles or visit airline websites to find out how to donate miles online.

An alternative to this idea that works better for me is:
_____
_____

May 30

Remove the foil from your oven.

Covering your oven racks with foil might make cleanup easier, but it also uses more energy. Foil reduces the heat flow, forcing your oven to work harder to cook your casserole. Reduced heat flow also increases cooking time, so skip the aluminum foil and clean up any messy spills with a damp cloth and a little elbow grease.

An alternative to this idea that works better for me is:
_____
_____

May 31

Pull weeds by hand.

If you have a garden, you probably have weeds. Pulling them the old-fashioned way—by hand—does take more work, but it is much more environmentally friendly than dousing them with harsh chemicals. A hand trowel or small hoe might make the job easier.

Pull weeds when the ground is moist and spread a thin layer of mulch, which will shade the surface of the garden and prevent weeds from germinating. Be sure to add the weeds to your compost pile.

An alternative to this idea that works better for me is:

_____

_____

June 1

Pick up dog waste with biodegradable scoop bags.

Your dog's waste might be biodegradable, but the plastic bags that you pick it up with are not. It can take up to 100 years for plastic dog-waste bags to decompose. There is an environmentally friendly solution: biodegradable scoop bags. You can toss them into the trash without worrying about their impact on the environment.

An alternative to this idea that works better for me is:

_____

_____

June 2

Schedule your errands back-to-back.

Driving to the post office in the morning, the dry cleaner in the afternoon, and the supermarket in the evening burns a lot of gas. Starting a car with a warm engine causes five times *less* pollution than starting a car with a cold engine. You can make your errands more eco-friendly by scheduling them back-to-back, instead of over several days (or a week). You'll keep the engine warm, cutting down on harmful emissions. Making fewer trips will also help you save money on gas.

An alternative to this idea that works better for me is:
_____
_____

June 3

Recycle your aluminum foil.

The aluminum foil you used to grill corn on the cob for dinner doesn't have to be relegated to the garbage. Just like soda cans, aluminum foil can be recycled. If the foil is coated with food, simply rinse it under cold water before putting it in the recycle box.

Check with your local waste-management company to make sure aluminum foil is recyclable in your area. If the answer is no, you can still make a greener choice: look for foil made from 100 percent recycled content. Manufacturing recycled foil requires just 5 percent of the energy of original processing.

An alternative to this idea that works better for me is:

June 4

Use an old, clean sock to dust your house.

If every household in the United States replaced just one roll of virgin fiber paper towels, we would save 544,000 trees a year! You can put a cotton sock over your hand and do all of your dusting without any waste. Once your housework is done, throw the sock in the washing machine and use it again and again.

An alternative to this idea that works better for me is:
_____
_____

June 5

Remove the screensaver from your computer.

A screensaver uses 100 watts of power, compared with just 10 watts in sleep mode. Consider this: a company with 5,000 computers that have screensavers running 20 hours per week uses emissions totaling 750,000 pounds of carbon dioxide, more than 5,800 pounds of sulfur oxide, and 1,500-plus pounds of nitrogen oxide per year.

An alternative to this idea that works better for me is:

_____

_____

June 6

Replace your plastic shower curtain liner.

Most shower curtain liners are made from polyvinyl chloride or PVC, a material that emits harmful gases that can cause cancer and diabetes. You might be breathing in toxins every time you take a shower. Choose a nylon shower curtain instead. Nylon is waterproof and contains no PVC. It is also washable, so when soap scum builds up, just toss it in the washing machine.

An alternative to this idea that works better for me is:

_____

_____

June 7

Schedule a yearly tune-up for your lawnmower.

Keeping your lawnmower in good working order will cut emissions by up to 50 percent and reduce fuel consumption by 30 percent. Most local hardware or home improvement stores offer lawnmower tune-up services.

An alternative to this idea that works better for me is:

_____

_____

June 8

Hang your clothes outside to dry.

The sunny skies and warmer temperatures offer the perfect opportunity to save energy. Dryers account for 6 percent of total electricity consumed in the United States and cost an average of $80 per year to operate. Using a clothesline will cut back on your energy consumption and leave your clothes smelling as fresh as a summer day. Continue saving energy in the winter months by investing in a drying rack.

Some homeowners associations don't allow residents to hang clotheslines. Check the rules of your HOA before stringing a line in your backyard.

An alternative to this idea that works better for me is:

_____

_____

June 9

Wipe down the vents in your central air conditioner.

Dust collects in the vents over the winter and gets blown into the air the first time the air conditioning is turned on every season. Keep dust particles and other allergens from being blasted through your home by taking a few minutes to wipe down the vents with a damp cloth.

An alternative to this idea that works better for me is:

_____

_____

June 10

Repair your leaky faucet.

Leaky faucets can waste up to 20 gallons of water per day. Stop the dripping—and conserve water—by replacing the washer. It's a simple fix that will cost a few dollars. If you're not comfortable doing it yourself, call a professional.

An alternative to this idea that works better for me is:
_____
_____

June 11

Avoid preheating the oven too soon.

It takes a lot of energy to preheat the oven; the longer the oven is turned on but not used, the more energy it wastes. Your oven only needs a few minutes to reach the desired temperature, so heat it when you're ready to make dinner, not 30 minutes before. If you bake twice a week, you can save almost 50 pounds of carbon per year by not preheating the oven earlier than necessary.

An alternative to this idea that works better for me is:

_____

_____

June 12

Use ice to sharpen the blades in your garbage disposal.

Instead of using food waste like peach pits to sharpen garbage disposal blades, use ice. Ice is safer because it won't harm aquatic life when it reaches streams and lakes.

An alternative to this idea that works better for me is:

_____

_____

June 13

Reserve a plot in a community garden.

Growing your own fruits and vegetables is possible, even if you live in an apartment. Join a community garden. Community gardens charge a small fee for a plot where you can grow everything from tomatoes and beans to melons and blueberries. You'll have the chance to dig in the dirt while improving the neighborhood and connecting to the environment.

There are more than 5,000 community gardens across the United States. You can find a community garden near you by going to www.communitygarden.org.

An alternative to this idea that works better for me is:

_____

_____

June 14

Turn up the temperature on your air conditioner.

Try keeping the temperature set to 78 degrees throughout the summer to save energy and reduce your cooling costs. You'll cut your cooling costs by up to 10 percent for every degree you raise your thermostat.

If all U.S. households raised the temperature on their thermostat by just 6 degrees, it would save the equivalent of 190,000 barrels of oil per day!

An alternative to this idea that works better for me is:

_____

_____

June 15

Make a list of the items you can borrow this summer.

If you're going to need a chainsaw or punch bowl, borrow them instead of buying them brand new. It's an especially good idea if you're borrowing things you only use occasionally. Instead of shelling out big bucks for specialty tools, you can rent them at most home improvement centers. Borrowing will save you a lot of money and help you conserve resources.

An alternative to this idea that works better for me is:

_____

_____

June 16

Aerate your lawn.

Aerating is one of the simplest things you can do to improve the overall health of your lawn. It boosts oxygen supply to the roots, improves water absorption, and allows nutrients to penetrate the soil. Aeration also breaks up compacted soil, releases carbon dioxide, and encourages deeper root growth. Your lawn should be aerated twice a year (spring and fall are the best times to aerate). You might have to aerate more often if you have clay soil or excessive thatch buildup. You can rent a power aerator from your local home improvement center or hire someone to do the job.

An alternative to this idea that works better for me is:

_____

_____

June 17

Write a letter to your senator.

Members of Congress care about the viewpoints of their constituents and take their feedback into account when it's time to vote. Your letter could help influence their vote on issues ranging from expanding local recycling programs to drilling in the Arctic National Wildlife Refuge. Get tips for writing a letter to your senator at www.pfaw.org.

An alternative to this idea that works better for me is:

_____

_____

June 18

Store leftovers in glass containers instead of plastic.

Plastic storage containers are manufactured using a chemical called bisphenol-A (BPA). The toxic substance is released as plastics age and when they are washed or heated. It contaminates the foods it comes into contact with and can cause health problems like obesity and hyper-activity as well as problems with reproductive cycles.

An alternative to this idea that works better for me is:

_____

_____

June 19

Get rid of garden pests naturally.

Natural pest control is almost always as effective as chemical pesticides. More importantly, it does not harm the environment. The residue from chemical pesticides eventually ends up in lakes and rivers where it can be ingested by local wildlife. Harsh chemicals can also kill beneficial insects that actually help the garden.

In most cases, a mixture of soap and warm water will take care of garden pests. Mix two teaspoons of dishwashing liquid with one quart of warm water and spray the infected plants liberally. If slugs are a problem, you can use a natural remedy like beer to get rid of them (see May 5).

Ladybugs, spiders, praying mantises, and wasps all eat insects that destroy plants. You can attract spiders by applying a thin layer of mulch in the spring, giving them a cool and dark place to live. Most garden centers sell ladybugs and praying mantises that can be relocated to your garden for natural pest control.

Plants like herbs and clover will also attract beneficial insects, so try integrating them into your flowerbeds this spring.

An alternative to this idea that works better for me is:
_____
_____

June 20

Pack your lunch in an insulated lunch bag.

Plastic bags never fully decompose, and it takes almost 12 million barrels of oil to manufacture the 100 billion plastic bags that Americans use every year. Paper bags might be recyclable, but the manufacturing process produces 50 times more water pollutants and 70 times more air pollutants than the manufacture of plastic bags. An insulated lunch bag can be used over and over again without any waste. And unlike paper or plastic bags, an insulated lunch bag will keep your sandwiches and soda cool.

An alternative to this idea that works better for me is:
_____
_____

June 21

Research real-estate agents who understand the importance of green building.

A real-estate agent certified by EcoBroker International is educated in issues like indoor air quality, energy-efficient technology, and sustainable design. Since the program was launched in 2003, more than 1,700 agents have signed on to help buyers interested in finding a green home.

An alternative to this idea that works better for me is:
_____
_____

June 22

Clean the lint screen in your dryer before each use.

The lint that collects in the filter prevents air from flowing efficiently through the dryer, forcing it to work harder to dry your clothes. Cleaning the lint screen can reduce your energy use by up to 30 percent. More importantly, it can also prevent a fire from starting in your dryer.

An alternative to this idea that works better for me is:

June 23

Wash your car at a commercial carwash.

You'll use between 80 and 140 gallons of water to wash your car at home, compared with just 45 gallons of water at a commercial carwash. Most commercial carwashes also have wastewater-management systems so water contaminated with chemical soaps is not discharged directly into the sewer system. If you must wash your car at home, use a biodegradable soap specifically formulated for automotive parts.

An alternative to this idea that works better for me is:

_____

_____

June 24

Put a cover on your pool.

Pool covers reduce heat loss and can cut water evaporation by up to 90 percent. Leaving your pool uncovered is just like turning on the air conditioning full blast and leaving the windows and doors open.

An alternative to this idea that works better for me is:

_____

_____

June 25

Read magazines at the library instead of buying them.

It takes more than 15 trees to manufacture one ton of high-quality, coated paper used to print magazine pages. Reading them in the library is free and will save valuable resources.

An alternative to this idea that works better for me is:

_____

_____

June 26

Design your garden to take advantage of storm-water runoff.

Rain gardens are built near driveways and rooftops to capture the rainwater that would otherwise end up flowing into storm drains. Compared to a regular patch of lawn, a rain garden allows about 30 percent more water to soak into the ground, which prevents erosion, water pollution, and flooding.

You can build your own rain garden using common nursery products and a little elbow grease. Choose an area where storm-water runoff accumulates (underneath the eaves and alongside the driveway are good choices) and install a layer of gravel beneath the soil to improve drainage.

Native plants are the best option for rain gardens because they are more tolerant of the local climate and soil and water conditions, and they require little fertilizer. Talk to a professional at your neighborhood garden center about which plants are native to your area. In most cases, a combination of ferns, wildflowers, and sedge grass is a good choice.

An alternative to this idea that works better for me is:

_____

_____

June 27

Invite friends to a summer barbeque using electronic invites.

You can e-mail invitations using websites like www.evite.com and www.sendomatic.com. Electronic invitations eliminate paper waste and save you money on stationery and postage costs. If paper invites are a must, choose invitations made from 100 percent recycled paper.

An alternative to this idea that works better for me is:

_____

_____

June 28

Pack a waste-free lunch.

Eliminate plastic bags, disposable containers, paper napkins, and plastic utensils from your lunch. You might be tempted to buy convenience foods in single-serving packages at the supermarket, but the waste adds up quickly. Over 10 billion yogurt cups and 3.6 billion drink pouches end up in the landfill every year. Try packing a waste-free lunch. Seal your sandwich in a reusable container, fill a thermos with soup, use a cloth napkin, and pack it all in a reusable lunch bag.

An alternative to this idea that works better for me is:

June 29

Skip the plastic stir stick with your morning cup of coffee.

The plastic stir sticks you use to mix cream and sugar into your coffee end up in the landfill. In fact, Americans throw away 138 billion straws and stirrers every year. You can mix your coffee without the stir stick; just pour the sugar in first, and then add the milk or cream. It will create a splash in the cup, stirring up the coffee.

An alternative to this idea that works better for me is:

_____

_____

June 30

Switch to eco-friendly cat litter.

Over 2 million tons of non-biodegradable cat litter ends up in the landfill every year. Traditional cat litter is made from clay using a process called strip-mining. Strip-mining uses heavy equipment to remove the top layer of earth to get to buried clay. It has destroyed thousands of acres of land and removed millions of tons of soil. Choose cat litter made from wheat, recycled newspaper, corn cobs, or other renewable materials that are biodegradable or easily composted.

An alternative to this idea that works better for me is:

_____

_____

July 1

Make a few eco-friendly changes to keep mosquitoes at bay.

You don't need a bug zapper or harsh chemicals to control mosquitoes. Standing water in your yard is a breeding ground for mosquitoes. Drill holes in the bottom of your plant pots, recycling bins, and trash cans and be sure to replace the water in birdbaths, water fountains, and pet bowls regularly to prevent mosquitoes from laying eggs.

An alternative to this idea that works better for me is:

July 2

DONE ◯

Serve dinner on dishes that can be composted.

Your friends and family will eat a lot of hot dogs and corn on the cob this summer. Instead of using paper plates, opt for dinnerware that can be composted. You can find plates, cups, and utensils made of organic sugarcane at most natural-foods stores. When it's time to clean up, just toss the plates into the compost pile. You'll help keep more than 100 billion plastic, paper, and Styrofoam cups from the landfills every year.

An alternative to this idea that works better for me is:

_____

_____

July 3

Store a solar charger in the glove compartment of your car.

Take advantage of the sunny skies by keeping a solar charger in your car. You can charge your cell phone, digital camera, and MP3 player without using any electricity. It's a great option to keep your electronics charged for a day at the beach. A solar charger is also a great accessory for foreign travel because it eliminates the worry about voltage converters. Solar chargers are sold at electronics stores for about $30.

An alternative to this idea that works better for me is:

July 4

Celebrate Independence Day without fireworks.

Fireworks wreak havoc on the environment. The fallout from fireworks displays causes toxic pollution that infiltrates soil and groundwater. Fireworks are also filled with heavy metals like cadmium, lithium, and lead. Barium, a chemical used to produce brilliant green colors in fireworks, is both poisonous and radioactive; copper, an element used to make blue fireworks, contains dioxin, which has been linked to cancer. Instead of watching fireworks displays on the Fourth of July, celebrate by going to a parade or hosting a block party.

An alternative to this idea that works better for me is:
_____
_____

July 5

Turn on the air conditioning in your car.

Keeping the windows open might seem like the eco-friendly option, but it actually reduces the aerodynamics of the car, making it less fuel efficient, especially on the highway. You'll actually improve your fuel economy by 20 percent or more if you drive with the A/C on and the windows rolled up. As a bonus, you'll be a lot cooler when you arrive at your destination.

An alternative to this idea that works better for me is:

July 6

Start a compost pile in your backyard.

Composting food waste such as apple cores and coffee grounds helps divert it from the landfill, prevents erosion, and keeps pollutants from leaching into the water. Compost enhances the nutrient content in soil, encourages the production of beneficial microorganisms, and acts as a natural fertilizer.

> If you're eager to produce compost quickly, try turning the pile weekly. It will improve air circulation and speed up the compost process. You can also shred organic materials before adding them to the pile to help them break down faster.

Composting is simple: all you need is a compost pile (an unused corner of the backyard is a perfect location) and patience. Add organic material such as grass clippings and food scraps to the pile, and wait for it to decompose. It can take up to a year for the material on the bottom of the pile to turn into rich compost material. Once it does, add it to your garden beds and watch your plants thrive.

An alternative to this idea that works better for me is:
_____
_____

July 7

Leave the grass clippings on your lawn.

Yard waste (including grass clippings) accounts for 50 percent of the waste sent to the landfill during the summer months.

Grass clippings break down easily and add nitrogen and other nutrients to the soil, cutting down on fertilizer use. Leftover grass clippings also stimulate earthworm activity, which reduces thatch, a tightly packed cluster of grasses in your lawn that prevents water and air from reaching the roots of your grass. You'll be reducing waste and enjoying a lush green lawn without any effort at all.

An alternative to this idea that works better for me is:

_____

_____

July 8

Slather on organic sunscreen.

Sunscreen is essential if you spend time outside in the summer sun. But the same ingredients that help protect you against UV exposure might be harming fish. Fish ingest the chemicals in your sunscreen that wash off when you're swimming. Opt for sunscreens that are labeled "organic" and "biodegradable" to protect yourself and the environment.

An alternative to this idea that works better for me is:

_____

_____

July 9

Spend the afternoon at the farmers market.

You can show your support for local growers by shopping at the farmers market. You'll find an array of locally grown fruits and vegetables, homemade preserves, baked goods, flowers, plants, and crafts. The produce sold at the farmers market is grown on nearby farms and harvested at its peak to ensure freshness. Farmers markets are also an excellent source of organic produce. Take time to sample the products and talk to the farmers about how their produce was grown.

An alternative to this idea that works better for me is:

_____

_____

July 10

Toss your used coffee grounds in the garden.

Coffee grounds make excellent fertilizer for nitrogen-loving plants like roses, azaleas, and blueberries. Sprinkle the grounds around your plants before you water to create an instant slow-release fertilizer. You can also add coffee grounds to your compost pile (see July 6).

Not a coffee drinker? Ask your barista to save used coffee grounds; your garden will thank you.

An alternative to this idea that works better for me is:

_____

_____

July 11

Save your shower water.

A shower uses up to 50 gallons of water. You could let the water run down the drain, or you could save it to water your plants. Plug the drain and let the water pool in the bathtub. After your shower, use a container to scoop up the water and pour it over the thirsty plants in your garden.

An alternative to this idea that works better for me is:

_____

_____

July 12

Research eco-friendly wood furnishings.

Shopping for the perfect coffee table or dining-room chairs takes time: you want to find a piece that looks great and fits your budget. It's also important to ensure that the wood used to make your furniture did not come from an endangered forest.

Look for furniture that has been certified by the Forest Stewardship Council (FSC). It's an international organization providing certification for wood-based products that were made using eco-friendly practices.

Lowe's Home Improvement Centers and Home Depot stock FSC-certified products. You can also contact local retailers to ask if they carry furniture made from sustainably harvested wood.

An alternative to this idea that works better for me is:

_____

_____

July 13

Look around the house for things that can be repaired.

"Repair" is considered the fourth "R" in reduce, reuse, and recycle. You probably have items around the house—a television, vacuum cleaner, or favorite pair of boots—that could be repaired instead of being tossed in the trash. Gather all your repairable items together and then go online to find repair shops in your area. Repairing items you currently own is much cheaper than buying brand-new replacement items, and keeps items out of the landfill.

An alternative to this idea that works better for me is:

_____

_____

July 14

Get the junk out of your trunk.

If you're driving around with the cooler, beach chairs, and charcoal grill from your vacation in your trunk, you're not getting good gas mileage. An extra 100 pounds in the trunk can reduce your car's fuel efficiency by up to 2 percent, so take the time to store the gear in the garage.

You can also boost your fuel mileage by removing the roof rack. The extra weight and the aerodynamic drag on the car both negatively affect your fuel efficiency.

An alternative to this idea that works better for me is:
_____
_____

July 15

Buy refillable beauty products.

Plastics such as shampoo bottles take up 25 percent of the space in landfills. Instead of buying a new bottle of shampoo, conditioner, body lotion, or liquid soap every time you run out, look for products that can be refilled. Natural product retailers often encourage their customers to bring in their empty bottles for a refill. Bonus: you'll get a discount for your recycling ways!

An alternative to this idea that works better for me is:

_____

_____

July 16

Borrow a DVD from the library or rent one from the video store, rather than buying something you might not want to rewatch.

Manufacturing a DVD requires a combination of nonrenewable resources like aluminum and nickel as well as polycarbonate, a type of plastic made from crude oil and natural gas.

In the United States, more than 100,000 DVDs are thrown away every month. DVDs cannot be recycled, so the waste ends up in the landfill. You can help cut down on waste and reduce the environmental impact of manufacturing DVDs by renting or borrowing your favorite movies instead of buying them. If you do own DVDs, donate them to a local library or thrift store instead of throwing them in the garbage.

An alternative to this idea that works better for me is:

July 17

Try the 100-mile diet.

On average, the ingredients you use to make your favorite meal travel 1,500 miles before they reach your plate. The abundance of fresh fruits and veggies available in the summer makes it the perfect time to try the 100-mile diet—eating foods that were grown within 100 miles of your home. You can try it for a single meal, an entire day, or longer. In the process, you'll learn more about local food sources and which foods are in season. Who knows, you might even discover a new favorite vegetable! Learn more about the 100-mile diet at www.100milediet.com.

An alternative to this idea that works better for me is:

_____

_____

July 18

Use a funnel to top off your car's motor oil to prevent spills.

Motor oil that lands on your driveway instead of in the oil pan gets washed into the storm drain and makes its way into rivers and streams.

Used motor oil is the largest single source of water pollution in the United States. More than 180 million gallons of used oil ends up in rivers and streams every year—16 times the amount of oil spilled by the *Exxon Valdez*. When the oil reaches the water, it doesn't dissolve. Instead, it sticks to everything from beach sand to bird feathers. Even worse, motor oil is toxic to plants and wildlife.

> The oil tanker *Exxon Valdez* was bound for Washington State on March 24, 1989, when it hit the Bligh Reef in Prince William Sound and spilled an estimated 10.8 million gallons of crude oil into its waters. It was one of the largest oil spills—and ecological disasters—in U.S. history.

An alternative to this idea that works better for me is:

_____

_____

DONE ○

July 19

Run your pool filter and sweeper system over-night.

Cleaning your pool during off-peak hours (like the middle of the night) helps conserve energy. During peak hours, power companies are often forced to use backup generators to meet the demand for energy. Backup generators are not as efficient as the main generators, so you're actually using more energy to do the same amount of work. Running your pool filter (and other appliances) during off-peak hours minimizes the need for backup power generators, which are often bigger polluters than main generators.

An alternative to this idea that works better for me is:

_____

_____

July 20

Check your toilet for leaks.

A leaky toilet can waste between 300 and 60,000 gallons of water per month, depending on the severity of the leak. If it's a slow leak, you might not even notice it.

Put a few drops of food coloring in the toilet tank (on the back of the toilet where the flushing mechanism is located). Wait 30 minutes and then check the toilet bowl. If the food coloring is in the toilet bowl, you have a leak and it's time to call a plumber.

An alternative to this idea that works better for me is:

_____

_____

July 21

Put garbage where it belongs—in the trash can.

It might be tempting to flush cigarette butts and dead bugs down the toilet, but each time you flush, you use up to six gallons of water. It takes more energy to dispose of unnecessary objects like Q-tips and razor blades at the sewage treatment plant. You should also avoid flushing diapers and sanitary products. You're likely to clog the toilet and could end up using more water attempting to flush bulky items like these. If you must put facial tissue in the toilet, wait until the next time you go to the bathroom before flushing.

An alternative to this idea that works better for me is:

_____

_____

July 22

Turn off the lights.

Your mom was right: there is no reason to leave the lights on after you leave the room. Nearly 15 percent of your annual electricity bill goes toward lighting your house. In the summer, turning the lights off will also keep the house cooler, so be sure to flip the switch when you leave the room.

An alternative to this idea that works better for me is:

_____

_____

July 23

Close your doors and windows if the air conditioning is on.

Your A/C will work overtime to cool your house if you forget to close your windows and doors. Before you leave the house, go from room to room to double-check that the cool air isn't escaping outside through an open window. In just a few minutes, you can dramatically cut your energy costs.

An alternative to this idea that works better for me is:

_____

_____

July 24

Have a yard sale.

You may not need the used baby clothes and romance novels that have been gathering dust in your garage, but someone else might. A yard sale will help keep gently used items from the landfill and allow you to make a few dollars in the process. You can up your ecological impact by donating the proceeds from the yard sale to your favorite green organization.

A yard sale is a good option for inexpensive household goods. Consider taking big-ticket items to a consignment store or auction house.

An alternative to this idea that works better for me is:

_____

_____

July 25

Give your breakfast to the birds!

Instead of tossing stale bagels in the trash, tie a piece of string around the bagel and hang it in a tree. Birds—and the occasional squirrel—will flock to your yard for breakfast. Best of all, there is no waste; the entire treat is edible.

> Spread peanut butter on the bagel and roll it in birdseed to give the birds an extra treat.

An alternative to this idea that works better for me is:

_____

_____

July 26

Turn your car off while you wait.

When you're picking up the kids at summer camp, turn off your car. For every minute your car idles, it emits almost 7 grams of pollutants like nitrous oxides and carbon dioxide into the atmosphere.

You can also save gas by reducing excessive idling: for every 10 minutes you let your vehicle idle, you use approximately 25 gallons of gas per year. If 10 percent of the U.S. population avoided idling for 5 minutes per day, we could lessen CO_2 emissions by 1 million tons and save more than 422,000 gallons of gas every year.

An alternative to this idea that works better for me is:

July 27

Explore alternatives to fabric softener.

Most liquid fabric softeners contain ammonium chloride, which can harm marine life. You can keep these harmful chemicals from entering the wastewater system by replacing liquid fabric softener with a natural alternative. Try pouring a quarter cup of white vinegar or a quarter cup of baking soda (but not both) into the rinse cycle. White vinegar or baking soda will soften your clothes naturally without any unpleasant odors.

An alternative to this idea that works better for me is:

July 28

Recycle your milk and juice cartons.

The average American consumes more than 3,200 half gallons of milk during their lifetime, but just 2 percent of the paper cartons are re-cycled. It takes more than one *trillion* kilowatt hours of energy and more than 740 million tons of greenhouse gases to manufacture, ship, and provide landfill space for that many milk cartons. The same amount of energy could power New York City for 16 years!

An alternative to this idea that works better for me is:
_____
_____

July 29

Keep a garment bag in your car to deliver your dry cleaning.

The plastic bags your dry cleaner uses to wrap your clean clothes eventually end up in the landfill. Unlike the thin plastic covering, a garment bag can be reused every time you take your clothes to the cleaners. Ask your dry cleaner to skip the plastic wrap and return your clothes in your (reusable) garment bag. Most dry cleaners will be happy to oblige.

> Store a garment bag in your car so you'll always have it on hand when you drop off your clothes.

An alternative to this idea that works better for me is:

July 30

Donate your old eyeglasses to those in need.

The prescription glasses you no longer wear can give the gift of sight to the visually impaired in developing countries. Lions Clubs (www.lionsclubs.org), Goodwill Industries (http://locator.goodwill.org), and LensCrafters (www.lenscrafters.com) collect used eyeglasses, repair them, and distribute them around the world to those who can't afford to buy brand-new glasses. Go online to find out where to drop off your old glasses. Your glasses will go to those who need them instead of languishing in the landfill.

An alternative to this idea that works better for me is:

_____

_____

DONE

July 31

Cut back on copies at the office.

  In the United States, the average office worker uses approximately 10,000 sheets of copy paper per year. You can cut back on the amount of paper you use at work by e-mailing or posting documents instead of printing a copy for everyone in the office—and encourage your officemates to follow suit.

An alternative to this idea that works better for me is:
_____
_____

August 1

DONE
○

Create electronic to-do lists.

Instead of scribbling your grocery list on a piece of paper (or printing it off of the computer) e-mail it to your mobile device. You'll save a lot of paper and it'll never get lost at the bottom of your purse. Best of all, you'll have an electronic copy to refer to if necessary.

An alternative to this idea that works better for me is:

_____

_____

August 2

Make a note to monitor the thermostat in your hotel room.

While you're on vacation this summer, check the temperature in your hotel room. If there is an in-room thermostat, set it just as you would at home: adjust the temperature when you go out so you're not blasting the air conditioning while no one is in the room. You can readjust the temperature when you return to the room.

An alternative to this idea that works better for me is:

_____

_____

August 3

Switch to an all-natural dishwasher detergent.

Your dishwasher detergent probably contains petroleum-based products. Petroleum, made from the same crude oil used to manufacture gasoline, is a known carcinogen. Opt for vegetable-based dishwasher detergent; the soap is milder and made from all-natural ingredients.

> If every household in the United States replaced one 25-ounce bottle of petroleum-based dishwasher detergent with a 25-ounce vegetable-based product, it would save 81,000 barrels of oil—enough to heat and cool 4,600 homes for an entire year!

An alternative to this idea that works better for me is:
_____
_____

August 4

Put a lid on your pots and pans.

When you're making dinner, cover your pots and pans to keep heat from escaping. The heat from the burner that enters the bottom of the pan will exit through the top if the pot isn't covered. It takes about half the time (and energy) to boil water in a covered pot.

An alternative to this idea that works better for me is:

August 5

Find out how to dispose of the hazardous waste in your garage.

The average garage has about 100 pounds of household hazardous waste. Products like paint, car-care products, and fertilizer can't be tossed in the trash. Most cities have special collection events several times per year to ensure that your hazardous waste doesn't end up in the landfill. Go to www.earth911.org/household-items to find out how to dispose of hazardous waste in your area.

An alternative to this idea that works better for me is:
_____
_____

August 6

Come up with a list of ideas for green gifts.

A batch of homemade chocolate chip cookies, a jar of homemade preserves, or a bouquet of fresh flowers from your garden makes a great birthday present or housewarming gift. Edible and perishable gifts result in little, if any, waste. Best of all, the recipient knows the gift came from the heart.

An alternative to this idea that works better for me is:

_____

_____

August 7

Switch to recycled toilet paper.

Recycled toilet paper uses less energy and fewer natural resources to produce; it's also comparable in price to non-recycled brands. Look for brands that are unbleached to help keep harmful chemicals from being released into wastewater during the manufacturing process.

If every household in the United States replaced one four-pack of toilet paper with a recycled brand, it would save 988,000 trees and 356 million gallons of water. It would also prevent more than 60,600 pounds of chlorine pollution.

An alternative to this idea that works better for me is:

_____

_____

August 8

Purchase a refillable card or tokens for public transportation.

Taking the bus or train to work is a much greener option than driving, but the waste from those paper tickets can really add up. In most cities, you can buy tokens or plastic cards (like gift cards) that can be reloaded over and over again, totally eliminating the small scraps of paper that end up in the trash.

> If your city doesn't offer tokens or tickets, contact the transit company and ask them to consider implementing greener payment options.

An alternative to this idea that works better for me is:

_____

_____

August 9

Switch to natural toothpaste.

Your toothpaste is filled with hard-to-pronounce ingredients like polyethylene glycol, methylparaben, and triclosan that are bad for your health and the environment.

Polyethylene is a suspected kidney toxin, methylparabens have been linked to breast cancer, and triclosan could cause birth defects and decrease fertility.

Eco-friendly toothpastes are made with natural ingredients like baking soda, spearmint, and tea tree oil that have no harmful side effects.

An alternative to this idea that works better for me is:
_____
_____

August 10

Pick up litter.

Do your part for the environment by taking a minute to pick up the plastic bag that landed on your lawn, the flyer blowing around the parking lot, or the aluminum can that was left on the playground. Litter dropped in the streets travels to waterways where it harms wildlife and pollutes the water supply. It only takes a moment to pick up a piece of litter but it has a huge impact on the environment.

An alternative to this idea that works better for me is:

_____

_____

August 11

Think twice before using your blow dryer.

The average hair dryer uses 45 kWh of energy a year—enough to burn a 60-watt light bulb for 3,259 hours. During the summer, when it's warm outside, letting your hair air dry will save a lot of energy.

On the days when you do use your hair dryer, be sure to unplug it when you're done so it's not using power needlessly.

An alternative to this idea that works better for me is:

_____

_____

August 12

Take the stairs instead of the elevator.

A 20-floor round trip on an elevator uses approximately 100 Wh of energy—the same amount of energy it takes to power a desktop computer for 30 minutes.

You're probably not going to walk 20 flights of stairs, but getting off of the elevator a few floors early—and encouraging your co-workers to do the same—adds up to a significant energy savings (not to mention the impact it'll have on your waistline).

An alternative to this idea that works better for me is:

_____

_____

August 13

Switch to eco-friendly dental floss.

Conventional dental floss is coated in chemical wax and sold in a plastic container. Look for brands that are made with vegetable wax or essential oil and packaged in cardboard, which can be recycled when the floss runs out.

An alternative to this idea that works better for me is:

_____

_____

August 14

Make new friends who care about the environment.

Social groups like Green Drinks and www.greensingles.com were designed to introduce people who care about the environment. Sign up and start making connections with others who value the planet.

An alternative to this idea that works better for me is:

_____

_____

August 15

Search for used sports equipment.

Need a tennis racket or bigger shoulder pads to play football? You can find great deals on used sporting equipment. Search newspaper ads, on-line forums, and resale stores to see if you can find used gear; you'll save money and keep sporting equipment from going to the landfill.

An alternative to this idea that works better for me is:

August 16

Research environmentally friendly courier services.

There might be alternatives to having a gas-guzzling truck deliver your packages. Look for a courier service that uses hybrid vehicles; if you need to schedule an in-town delivery, research bicycle couriers.

An alternative to this idea that works better for me is:
_____
_____

August 17

Use the most energy-efficient kitchen appliance.

Some kitchen appliances use less energy than others, so simply choosing the most efficient appliance can make a huge difference in your energy usage. You'll use 50 percent less energy by brewing your tea with an electric kettle instead of a stovetop model; a toaster oven uses half of the energy of a traditional convection oven. As a bonus, a toaster oven will also keep your house cooler during the summer months.

An alternative to this idea that works better for me is:

August 18

Throw a couple of clean tennis balls in the dryer to speed up drying time.

Tennis balls keep your clothes from sticking to the sides of the dryer. The more your damp clothes tumble around, the faster they'll dry.

There is another reason to put tennis balls in the dryer: it will help to fluff up items like comforters and pillows.

An alternative to this idea that works better for me is:

_____

_____

August 19

DONE
○

Ask about flex time at work.

Working four 10-hour days will cut your fuel consumption by 20 percent.

In 2007, 3,609 employees at the U.S. Patent and Trademark Office (USPTO) participated in a telecommuting program. Based on their calculations, USPTO employees who are allowed to work from home up to four days a week have helped save 613,000 gallons of fuel, prevented 9,600 tons of CO_2 emissions, and cut $1.8 million per year in fuel costs by allowing staff to work at home.

An alternative to this idea that works better for me is:

August 20

Turn off your iron!

Your iron uses as much energy as 10 100-watt light bulbs.

Cut back on energy use by removing clothes from the dryer immediately to prevent wrinkles. You can also hang your clothes in the bathroom when you shower; the steam from the shower will help remove wrinkles.

An alternative to this idea that works better for me is:

_____

_____

August 21

Make plans to carpool to Ramadan celebrations.

You'll cut down on fuel consumption and air pollution by carpooling. Invite family and friends to ride with you (and be sure to drive the most fuel-efficient vehicle)!

An alternative to this idea that works better for me is:

_____

_____

August 22

Shop online for back-to-school clothes.

Online shopping is more convenient and better for the environment. On average, e-commerce warehouses use $\frac{1}{16}$ the energy of a bricks-and-mortar store. Each minute spent driving to the mall uses 20 times more energy than a minute spent shopping online. When it's time to choose a shipping option for your online purchases, ground shipping is the greenest option.

An alternative to this idea that works better for me is:

August 23

Think about planting a green roof.

Green roofs are essentially rooftop gardens. Plants like sedum, wildflowers, and native grasses planted on your roof can help reduce air pollution and storm-water runoff and provide a habitat for wildlife. You can install a green roof on your house, your shed, or even your doghouse for as little as $10/square foot. Go to www.greenroofs.org to find out if a green roof is right for you.

An alternative to this idea that works better for me is:

August 24

Get an ID tag for your pet.

It takes a lot of resources to search for a lost pet. Most pet owners will spend hours driving around the neighborhood and post dozens of flyers in the hopes of finding their pet. An ID tag might not prevent your pet from getting lost, but it will increase the chances that he'll be returned home quickly.

An alternative to this idea that works better for me is:

August 25

Write it down on an erasable whiteboard.

Writing your to-do list on an erasable white-board will keep you from using—and throwing away—countless sheets of memo paper. Once the tasks are complete, erase the whiteboard and start all over. Be sure to buy erasable markers without toxic chemicals. Look for water-based markers that are xylene-free.

An alternative to this idea that works better for me is:
_____
_____

August 26

Look for recycled school supplies.

Stock your backpack with notebooks, binders, and paper made from recycled materials. Choose school supplies with as little packaging as possible (30 percent of the waste in our landfills comes from product packaging) and buy in bulk, if possible. Go through last year's school supplies to see which items can be used again this year.

An alternative to this idea that works better for me is:

_____

_____

August 27

Research the most eco-friendly computers.

Take advantage of the back-to-school sales to upgrade to a more eco-friendly computer. Laptops use up to 50 percent less energy than traditional desktop computers. Look for a laptop with the Energy Star label; it's a government certification for energy efficiency.

Replace your old cathode ray tube (CRT) monitor with a monitor that has a liquid crystal display (LCD) screen. A 14-inch LCD monitor uses up to 75 percent less energy than a 14-inch CRT monitor.

There is another benefit to buying a laptop: since they're smaller than desktops, laptops use less packaging.

An alternative to this idea that works better for me is:
_____
_____

August 28

Sharpen your Number 2 pencils.

In most cases, refillable products are the most environmentally friendly choice. When it comes to pencils, though, the old-fashioned wooden ones are best. Most Number 2 pencils are made from reclaimed wood while refillable pencils are made of nonrenewable plastic; when they break, the plastic casings have to be thrown in the garbage. Wooden pencils are virtually waste-free because they can be sharpened over and over until they disappear.

An alternative to this idea that works better for me is:

_____

_____

August 29

Start shopping for used textbooks.

Used textbooks are much cheaper than brand-new volumes, but there is another reason to buy books secondhand: more than 20 million trees are cut down every year to manufacture books sold in the United States.

Schoolbooks account for $10 billion in annual sales. If 10 percent of those books were recycled, it would save enough money to cover the tuition at an Ivy League college for 30,715 students, not to mention the reduction in greenhouse gases used to manufacture and transport those books!

An alternative to this idea that works better for me is:

August 30

Switch to a cast-iron cooking pan.

The chemical used to create the nonstick coating in your favorite cooking pan is harmful to the environment. Perfluorooctanoic acid, or PFOA, has been linked to cancer and respiratory illnesses. The fumes that are released during the manufacturing process can be fatal to birds, and the chemical never breaks down in the landfill. Cast-iron pans are a bit more expensive but have no harmful health and environmental impacts.

An alternative to this idea that works better for me is:

August 31

Talk about green options for back-to-school transportation.

You can have a huge impact on the environment if you use public transportation or arrange a carpool or have your kids ride the school bus instead of driving them to school. Depending on how far it is to school, you might want to consider letting your kids ride their bikes or skateboards. A walking buddy is also a good option, especially if you can pair younger kids with an older student at the same school.

An alternative to this idea that works better for me is:

September 1

Plan an eco-friendly Labor Day getaway.

The beach is one of the most popular places to spend Labor Day weekend. Try to minimize your impact while you're soaking up the sun.

Every year, 14 billion pounds of trash are dumped in the ocean, and plastics account for up to 90 percent of all floating marine debris. Take a trash bag with you to contain food packaging and empty sunscreen bottles. Be sure not to leave any garbage behind; it could poison or choke marine life. While you're at the beach, pick up any trash you come across.

An alternative to this idea that works better for me is:

_____

_____

September 2

Lower the setting on your water heater.

Setting the thermostat to 120 degrees improves performance and reduces energy costs. In fact, each 10-degree reduction in water temperature can save 3 to 5 percent on your monthly bills.

Reducing the water temperature to 120 degrees also slows mineral buildup and prevents corrosion in your water heater and pipes. The result: a water heater that operates at its maximum efficiency.

The thermostat on a gas water heater is usually located near the bottom of the tank, on the gas valve. On electric water heaters, the thermostat is normally located behind a screw-on panel. Be sure to shut off the electricity to the water heater before opening the panel.

An alternative to this idea that works better for me is:

_____

_____

September 3

Make your grill a little greener.

Gas and propane grills are more eco-friendly than charcoal grills, which emit tiny pollutants into the air when they're lit. If you have a charcoal grill, use natural briquettes that are made without additives like coal dust. Avoid easy-to-light briquettes, because they've been soaked in gas-based lighter fluid and give off harmful fumes when they're lit.

> Never use a grill indoors. Outdoors, keep your grill at least 10 feet away from the house to prevent fires.

Take green grilling one step further by using an ethanol-based lighter fluid (for charcoal grills), which is less harmful to the planet than a traditional barbeque lighter.

An alternative to this idea that works better for me is:

September 4

Use the electric hand dryer in the public restroom.

Public restrooms often have paper towel dispensers and electric dryers; opt for the electric dryer if you have the choice. Electric dryers are twice as efficient as paper towels.

The electricity that powers the hand dryers generates greenhouse gas but the environmental impact is still smaller compared to the energy used to manufacture paper towels. Plus, paper towels are often made from virgin fibers, not recycled materials, and bleached with chlorine, which can pollute soil and groundwater.

An alternative to this idea that works better for me is:

September 5

Ask about switching to recycled paper at the office.

Your office already has a recycling program in place, right? Help your workplace take its recycling efforts one step further by talking to your office manager about stocking the printer, copier, and fax machine with 100 percent recycled paper. It's available at most office-supply stores and doesn't cost much more than virgin stock.

On average, an office with only 10 employees can help to recycle 100,000 pieces of paper per year. Every ton of paper that's recycled saves more than 3.3 cubic yards of landfill space.

An alternative to this idea that works better for me is:

_____

_____

September 6

DONE
◯

Research careers in environmental fields.

Whether you're considering a career change, helping your kids decide on a college major, or just interested in learning more about what others are doing to protect the environment, take some time to research eco-friendly fields.

Go to www.environmentalcareer.com to learn more about fields like environmental activism, eco-toxicology, and aquatic ecology.

An alternative to this idea that works better for me is:
_____
_____

September 7

Join Freecycle to find items you need or to get rid of items you no longer use.

The online network was created to reduce waste and keep household items from going to the landfills. More than 4 million members have joined, requesting items they need and offering their unused items like treadmills, cribs, piles of bricks, and aquariums—all for free. There are over 4,000 Freecycle groups across the country. Find the group nearest you by logging on to www.freecycle.org.

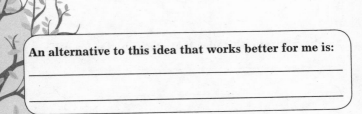

An alternative to this idea that works better for me is:

September 8

Keep the oven door closed when you're making dinner.

Resist the temptation to open the oven door to check on your pot roast. Each time you open the oven door, the temperature drops 25 to 50 degrees. It takes a lot of energy for the oven to regain the temperature losses, so if you have to peek, turn on the oven light and look through the glass.

An alternative to this idea that works better for me is:

_____

_____

September 9

Reschedule your sports matches.

It takes a lot of energy to light a sports field or tennis court. Instead of playing football or baseball in the evenings, try to schedule morning or afternoon matches. Lighting a single tennis court for a year requires more than 4,700 hours of energy—enough to power one U.S. home for six months.

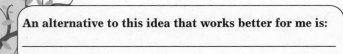

An alternative to this idea that works better for me is:

_____

_____

September 10

Scrape your dirty dishes before putting them in the dishwasher.

You can save up to 10 gallons of water by scraping the food off your dirty dishes instead of rinsing them. Scraping leftover food into the trash (or adding it to your compost pile; see July 6) also uses a lot less water than putting it in the garbage disposal.

> If every household in the United States scraped their dishes (and saved 10 gallons of water) tonight, it would save more than 1 billion gallons of water—*in just one day!*

An alternative to this idea that works better for me is:

_____

_____

September 11

Switch to non-aerosol cans.

You can find products ranging from household cleaners to hairspray in aerosol cans. A lot of aerosols use carbon dioxide, propane, and butane—greenhouse gases that contribute to global warming—to propel the product out of the can. Used aerosol cans are often considered hazardous waste because of the toxic propellants.

Non-aerosol cans are a more environmentally friendly alternative and readily available on store shelves. In most cases, you won't even have to switch products; just choose the non-aerosol versions of your favorite brands.

An alternative to this idea that works better for me is:

_____

_____

September 12

Ask your stylist about eco-friendly hair coloring.

Most hair dyes are made from synthetic and petroleum-based products that are harsh on your hair and bad for the environment. During the coloring process, hair dye is washed down the drain, making its way into groundwater and polluting wildlife habitat. Many salons offer eco-friendly dyes made with plant-based ingredients; talk to your stylist about alternatives to keep your hair looking great without harming the environment.

An alternative to this idea that works better for me is:

September 13

Buy baby food in glass jars.

You can reduce the amount of waste sent to the landfill by choosing baby food in glass jars. Every year, parents buy more than 1.4 billion units of baby food. Unlike plastic containers of pureed carrots and applesauce, glass jars can be recycled. The mini glass jars can also be reused for craft projects or storing small items like buttons or screws.

An alternative to this idea that works better for me is:
_____
_____

September 14

Buy a bigger jug of milk.

You can have a big impact on the environment by shopping for a gallon of milk instead of two half-gallon containers. In fact, it takes so much less energy to manufacture a bigger container, the average household could save enough energy to run a refrigerator for three days by shopping for a gallon—or more—of milk. Remember to put your empty milk jug in the recycle bin!

An alternative to this idea that works better for me is:
_____
_____

September 15

Say no to brochures and flyers.

Instead of accepting the brochures that are handed out at supermarkets, warehouse stores, and on street corners, decline the extra paper. Most of the details are available online; you're less likely to lose the information if it's stored on your computer instead of stuffed into the bottom of your purse or briefcase.

An alternative to this idea that works better for me is:

September 16

Buy a refillable pen.

Plastic pens are often made from nonrenewable petroleum products. During the manufacturing process, pens made from PVC plastic release
dioxins—the same chemical used to make Agent
Orange—into the environment. It takes fewer resources to manufacture refillable pens, and since
you can use the same pen over and over, there is
also less waste.

An alternative to this idea that works better for me is:
_____
_____

September 17

Think about skipping an oil change.

Your mechanic probably recommends having your oil changed every 3,000 miles, but most newer cars can go twice that long without service. Check your owner's manual to see what the manufacturer recommends. Chances are, unless you're racing down the freeway like a NASCAR driver, you can skip your next oil change.

Having your oil changed every 6,000 miles can have a huge impact on the environment: in California alone, 153 million gallons of oil are used every year. You can help cut that number in half by having your oil changed half as often.

An alternative to this idea that works better for me is:

_____

_____

September 18

Opt for a fountain drink instead of a bottle or can of soda.

Some restaurants will give you the choice between a fountain drink or a can or bottle of your favorite soda; choose the fountain drink.

In the United States, more than 100 billion aluminum cans and 22 billion plastic bottles are manufactured every year; only 51 percent of aluminum cans and 7 percent of plastic bottles are recycled. Soda from the fountain produces very little waste (especially if the restaurant serves your drink in a glass instead of a disposable cup), making it a more eco-friendly way to enjoy your favorite beverage.

An alternative to this idea that works better for me is:

September 19

Buff your leather shoes using an all-natural polish.

Commercial shoe polish is made of a toxic combination of turpentine and naphtha, a petroleum-based hydrocarbon. There are natural and inexpensive alternatives to keep your shoes looking brand new. Rub the inside of a banana peel over your shoes and then buff them with a clean cloth. Or use a bit of vegetable or olive oil on the leather until it's shiny.

> Check with your waste-management company before throwing out used shoe polish; in some areas it's considered hazardous waste and needs to be disposed of properly.

An alternative to this idea that works better for me is:

_____

_____

September 20

Put a full 20-ounce water bottle in your toilet tank for added weight.

Toilets manufactured before 1994 use at least 3.5 gallons of water with every flush (compared to 1.6 gallons/flush for low-flow models in newer homes).

Installing a low-flow toilet is a good option, but if it's not in your budget, consider putting a full water bottle inside the toilet tank. The added weight will create extra volume, reducing the amount of water it takes to refill the tank and using less water with every flush.

An alternative to this idea that works better for me is:

_____

_____

September 21

Play video games that offer environmental education.

Learning about the environment can be fun, even for kids who are glued to their video game consoles. Games like CO_2FX and SimCity Societies teach kids about global warming and environmental economics.

During a game of SimCity Societies, players have to decide between a coal plant, nuclear plant, wind plant, or solar plant to power their city; the decisions they make will impact other aspects of their virtual communities, including healthcare costs and real-estate values.

An alternative to this idea that works better for me is:

September 22

Replace your metal staplers with eco-staplers.

Tiny staples might not seem like a threat to the environment, but the little pieces of metal really add up. In the United States, more than 640,000 metric tons of staples are produced every year—and most of them end up in the trash.

During the manufacturing process, the heavy metals used to make staples can end up in the soil and groundwater where they are toxic to plants and wildlife.

A number of companies have started selling eco-staplers—small gadgets that bind up to five sheets of paper together without staples. You can find eco-staplers at most office-supply stores.

An alternative to this idea that works better for me is:

September 23

Evaluate your upcoming travel plans.

It's possible to have less of an impact on the environment by opting to take the train on your next vacation. A transcontinental flight generates 2.5 tons of carbon dioxide emissions; train travel creates between 4 and 15 percent of the CO_2 emissions (depending on the length of the trip). Bonus: you can avoid long lines at the airport and get a glimpse of parts of the country you could never see from the air.

An alternative to this idea that works better for me is:

_____

_____

September 24

Ditch your air freshener.

The same air freshener that makes your kitchen smell like a wildflower meadow is releasing toxins into the air every time you spray. Most air fresheners are made with chemicals like benzenes, phthalates, and formaldehyde.

Opt for natural alternatives like burning a beeswax candle, splurging on a bouquet of fresh flowers, or hanging dried lavender or eucalyptus throughout the house.

An alternative to this idea that works better for me is:

_____

_____

September 25

Buy some new crayons.

Crayons are often made of paraffin wax, a product made from nonrenewable petroleum sources. Some paraffin-based crayons might contain asbestos, a health and environmental hazard that helps strengthen the paraffin and bond the coloring agents. Instead, choose crayons made from soybean oil. Soy is a renewable resource that is completely biodegradable; it's also non-toxic, so you won't have to worry if the crayons end up in your child's mouth. Soy crayons are available almost everywhere crayons are sold.

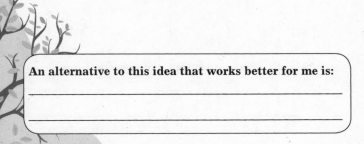

An alternative to this idea that works better for me is:

_____

_____

September 26

Reset the temperature in your refrigerator.

Your refrigerator accounts for 15 percent of the energy use in your home. The freezer should be set between 0 and 5 degrees and the refrigerator temperature should be between 37 and 40 degrees. You can also set the temperature dial (located inside the refrigerator) to the factory setting to ensure maximum energy efficiency.

An alternative to this idea that works better for me is:

_____

_____

September 27

Winterize your windows.

You don't have to replace your windows to take advantage of the latest energy-saving technology. Plastic film with low-E coating, an invisible layer of metallic oxide, helps reduce heat loss through old windows by up to 40 percent.

Home improvement stores sell low-E film for $3 to $12 per square foot. The self-adhesive film helps trap heat indoors during the winter. In less than one year, you'll save enough on your utility bills to cover the cost of the low-E coating.

An alternative to this idea that works better for me is:

_____

_____

September 28

Start saving your rainwater.

Install a rain barrel beneath your downspouts to help reduce storm-water runoff and conserve water. The water you collect in your rain barrel is also a good backup source during times of drought.

> Use the water that collects in the rain barrel for everything from watering the garden to bathing the dog—but remember not to drink it or use it for cooking.

You can purchase a small rain barrel at most home-improvement stores for as little as $50, or find instructions online to make your own. Be sure to choose a model with a secure lid to prevent children and animals from falling in and install a screened cover to keep mosquitoes from breeding in your rain barrel.

An alternative to this idea that works better for me is:
_____
_____

September 29

Wear an extra sweater.

As the temperatures start to cool, resist the urge to turn on the heat. Instead, use an age-old strategy to keep warm: wear an extra sweater. Keeping the thermostat turned off as long as possible will save a lot of energy (and keep your bills low).

An alternative to this idea that works better for me is:

_____

_____

September 30

Check your ducts for leaks.

Your ducts deliver hot air from the furnace to the rest of the house. Leaking ducts can increase heat loss by up to 30 percent, so it's a good idea to check your ducts before the cold weather arrives.

In most homes, the ducts are accessible in the basement, crawl space, or attic. First, check to see if the ducts have become disconnected; if this is the case, reconnect them. Next, turn on your heating system and feel for leaks. Seal any leaks with foil tape, which can be found at any home improvement store. (Duct tape, despite its name, is not a good choice for sealing leaks because the material deteriorates when it's exposed to hot air.)

The ducts in your home might not be easily accessible. If this is the case, it's best to hire a contractor to check for leaks.

An alternative to this idea that works better for me is:

October 1

Schedule a professional furnace inspection.

Your furnace should be inspected every year to ensure that it's in good working condition. A poorly maintained furnace may be only half as efficient as a furnace that is running well.

A qualified inspector can identify potential problems that are preventing your furnace from operating at peak efficiency. Look in the Yellow Pages or go online to find a qualified furnace inspector.

An alternative to this idea that works better for me is:

_____

_____

October 2

Seal drafts around your windows and doors.

You can keep your home warm and cozy—and cut your heating costs—by preventing heat escaping through your windows and doors.

To find leaks, light a candle and hold it in front of window and door seams. The flame will flicker in drafty spots.

Weather-stripping can help seal the drafts. Self-stick foam weather-stripping is the easiest to work with and should be installed on dry surfaces when temperatures are above 20 degrees. Simply measure the perimeter of the windows and doors and add 10 percent to the total to allow for waste and then follow the instructions on the package.

An alternative to this idea that works better for me is:

October 3

Shop for eco-friendly pet toys.

Your pets might never notice that their squeaky toys are made from recycled soda bottles, but you'll be keeping excess waste from going to the landfills. Look for hemp tug-of-war toys, chew toys made from recycled plastic, and pet beds stuffed with recycled materials.

The American Pet Products Manufacturers Association reports that pet owners spent $41.2 billion on their pets in 2007. You can send a message about the importance of eco-friendly pet products by purchasing treats and toys that have minimal environmental impact.

An alternative to this idea that works better for me is:

_____

_____

October 4

Plan a clothing swap.

Invite your friends over to swap the gently used clothes you no longer wear. You'll be able to "shop" for a new-to-you wardrobe and do your part to keep clothes from going to the landfill.

Over 4 million tons of all waste sent to the landfill is clothing and textiles. Synthetic fibers don't decompose, which means the polyester shirt you wore as a senior in high school will still be sitting in the landfill when you're a senior citizen.

An alternative to this idea that works better for me is:
_____
_____

October 5

Move your refrigerator.

Leaving space between your refrigerator and the wall increases air circulation around the condenser coils, allowing the fridge to operate more efficiently. If you have a freezer, be sure to move it away from the wall as well.

An alternative to this idea that works better for me is:

October 6

Sort your recyclables.

Resist the urge to toss your plastic milk jugs, aluminum soda cans, and shampoo bottles in the recycling bin without looking at the numbers on the bottles. There are several different grades of plastic, coded with numbers ranging from 1 to 7.

Some cities only recycle certain grades of plastic. Check with your local waste facility to find out which plastics can be recycled in your area. If you put a single bottle in the bin that your recycling facility can't accept, you risk contaminating the entire recycle bin. Too much contamination might mean a batch of recyclables is sent to the landfill instead.

An alternative to this idea that works better for me is:
_____
_____

October 7

Download software to send faxes electronically.

Send and receive faxes over the computer. Electronic faxing cuts down on the amount of paper you use and allows you to store important documents on your hard drive. Software can be downloaded for under $20 from websites like www.efax.com and www.faxit.com.

An alternative to this idea that works better for me is:

_____

_____

October 8

DONE ○

Call your mechanic to schedule a tune-up for your car.

Regular maintenance can improve your fuel efficiency by up to 20 percent. As part of the tune-up, your mechanic might install new spark-plugs, replace your air filter, and top off your motor oil. Fixing a serious maintenance problem like replacing a faulty oxygen sensor can improve gas mileage by up to 40 percent.

An alternative to this idea that works better for me is:

_____

_____

October 9

Switch to powdered laundry detergent.

Liquid laundry detergent is almost 80 percent water—a valuable, nonrenewable resource. If 20,000 Americans switched to powdered laundry detergent, it would save 55,000 gallons of water per year. You can have even more of an impact by switching to powdered dishwasher detergent, too.

An alternative to this idea that works better for me is:

October 10

Research eco-friendly builders and contractors.

Whether you're planning a green remodeling project or looking for a landscaping company to design a drought-tolerant garden, it's a good idea to do your research.

Check the U.S. Green Building Council (www.usgbc.org) or the Co-Op America Green Pages (www.coopamerica.org) for a list of eco-friendly contractors in your area.

An alternative to this idea that works better for me is:

_____

_____

October 11

Check your children's toys for lead.

A recent rash of toy recalls may have you wondering whether there is lead in the toy trucks and dolls your children love. Lead pollutes the air, soil, and water. It can also cause delays in growth and physical development, especially in children.

You can purchase lead-testing kits for less than $20. Simply swab your children's toys and wait for the results. If toys test positive for lead, don't throw them in the trash. Instead, call your local waste-management facility to find out how to dispose of them properly.

When you're shopping for new toys, chose unfinished wood or organic cotton. Or look for toys labeled lead-free.

An alternative to this idea that works better for me is:

_____

_____

October 12

Pay your bills online.

Paying bills online not only saves trees, it helps reduce greenhouse gas emissions by lessening the loads on trucks and planes delivering paper checks. If every household in the United States paid its bills online, it would cut waste by 1.6 billion tons a year and reduce greenhouse gas emissions by 2.1 million tons per year.

Ask your employer about depositing your paycheck into your account automatically instead of cutting you a check. You'll save paper and reduce fuel consumption by avoiding a trip to the bank every payday.

An alternative to this idea that works better for me is:
_____
_____

October 13

Adopt a highway.

Do your part to help the environment by sign-
ing up to keep a stretch of highway litter-free. As
part of the "adoption agreement," you promise to
help with the restoration of a local highway. You
can donate money to cleanup efforts, coordinate a
group of volunteers to pick up trash, or spend an
afternoon planting trees along a two-mile stretch
of road.

Your efforts will keep highways cleaner and
help prevent potential pollutants from entering
waterways. Volunteer efforts to clean up litter also
save taxpayers millions of dollars.

In most areas, it's free to adopt a highway. Go to
www.adoptahighway.com for more information.

An alternative to this idea that works better for me is:

_____

_____

October 14

Schedule a home energy audit.

Most utility companies offer free or low-cost in-home energy audits. The energy auditor will do a room-by-room evaluation of your home to evaluate how much energy you're using and offer suggestions for becoming more energy efficient. If your utility company doesn't offer energy audits, ask for referrals to a local expert.

An alternative to this idea that works better for me is:

_____

_____

October 15

Buy sugar and cream dispensers for your office.

The waste from the individual sugar packets and mini creamers in your office kitchen can really add up. Help your office become more eco-friendly by supplying a sugar jar and creamer (you can purchase them for a few dollars at a secondhand store) and asking your co-workers to chip in for bulk sugar and cartons of cream.

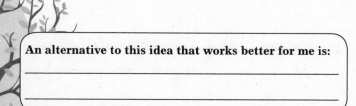

An alternative to this idea that works better for me is:

_____

_____

October 16

Switch to a manual can opener.

The electric can opener sitting on your kitchen counter only uses a little bit of energy (about .18 kWh per month for the average 175-watt brand), but electric can openers require more resources to manufacture, are more expensive to ship, and take up more space in the landfill. If everyone in the United States started using a manual can opener, it would save up to 648 million kWh of power.

An alternative to this idea that works better for me is:

_____

_____

October 17

Install a HEPA filter.

You can improve the indoor air quality in your home with a high-efficiency particulate air (HEPA) filter. The filters can trap more than 99 percent of airborne particles. HEPA filters that fit in your central heating and cooling system start at around $50.

An alternative to this idea that works better for me is:

_____

_____

October 18

Reuse plastic shopping bags.

You probably have dozens of plastic shopping bags lying around the house. Use them to line your garbage cans instead of buying a box of trash bags at the supermarket. For every ton of plastic bags that are reused, the energy equivalent of 11 barrels of oil is saved.

An alternative to this idea that works better for me is:

_____

_____

October 19

Buy refill packs of baby wipes.

Most baby wipes come in plastic packaging. You can cut down on waste by purchasing refill packs when you run out of baby wipes. The refill packs use 90 percent less packaging than the plastic containers of wipes, and result in less waste in the landfill.

An alternative to this idea that works better for me is:

_____

_____

October 20

Donate used winter coats to charity.

Don't toss your old winter coats in the trash. Instead, donate them to a homeless shelter. After you buy a new winter wardrobe, go through your closets and gather all of the coats, hats, and gloves you haven't worn in a while and donate them to charity instead of tossing them in the trash. According to the Environmental Protection Agency (EPA), Americans throw away more than 68 pounds of clothing and textiles *per person* per year. It's also the time of year to ask if shelters are in need of warm blankets.

An alternative to this idea that works better for me is:

_____

_____

October 21

Brainstorm ideas for an eco-friendly Halloween costume.

You don't have to buy a brand-new costume to look great on Halloween. Rent a costume, buy a secondhand costume at a thrift store, or raid your closet to come up with creative ideas. Pair a plaid shirt, old jeans, and a straw hat with a little face paint for an instant scarecrow costume.

> If you have children, consider organizing a costume swap with the neighbors. Your kids will get an almost-new costume that might have otherwise gone to the landfill.

An alternative to this idea that works better for me is:
_____
_____

October 22

Switch from an antiperspirant to a deodorant.

It's best to avoid antiperspirants because they contain aluminum salts, which help seal your pores to prevent sweating. It takes a significant amount of energy— an average of 7.5 kWh of electricity per pound—to mine aluminum. You can reduce your impact on the environment by switching to aluminum-free deodorant.

An alternative to this idea that works better for me is:
_____
_____

October 23

Clean your stove.

The burner liners under the burners in your stove reflect heat, helping foods cook faster. Burner liners that are covered with burnt-on foods decrease the energy efficiency of your stove. Remove the liners and scrub them well (or put them in the dishwasher). If it's impossible to remove the burnt-on food, buy new burner liners from a home improvement center.

An alternative to this idea that works better for me is:

October 24

Switch from a lighter to matches.

Over 1.5 billion lighters end up in the land-fill every year, where their plastic casings never break down. The plastic casings and butane fuel used in lighters are made from a petroleum-based source. Cardboard matchbooks are made from recycled paper, making them a greener choice for lighting the barbeque or your favorite candles.

An alternative to this idea that works better for me is:
_____
_____

October 25

Clean your gutters.

The leaves and debris that collect in your gutters mix with the rainwater and get washed down the sewer drain. Once the yard debris gets into the lakes and rivers, it creates algae, which decreases the oxygen in the water and kills marine life. After you've cleaned the gutters, add the yard debris to your compost pile or call your waste-management company to find out how to dispose of yard waste.

An alternative to this idea that works better for me is:
_____
_____

October 26

Leave your leaf blower in the garage.

Leaf blowers emit carbon monoxide, nitrogen oxide, and hydrocarbons. Two-stroke engines (like those in leaf blowers) cause as much smog as 17 cars every *hour* they're used! Rake your leaves instead. You'll get a good workout and keep pollutants, including noise pollution, from harming the environment.

An alternative to this idea that works better for me is:

_____

_____

October 27

Change the settings on your washer and dryer.

Unless you're washing delicates, use the fastest spin cycle on your washer. A fast spin will pull more water from your clothes so they'll be in the dryer for less time. A shorter drying time means you're using less energy.

On your dryer, use the moisture-sensing option (also called "auto dry" on some models) instead of the timed setting. The dryer will shut off automatically when your clothes are dry, eliminating excess drying time.

An alternative to this idea that works better for me is:

_____

_____

October 28

Stock your bathroom with bars of soap.

The scented body wash in your shower is packaged in a plastic container made of non-renewable, petroleum-based sources and uses a lot more packaging than a bar of soap.

If every household in the United States re-placed one bottle of body wash with a bar of soap, it would save almost 2.5 million pounds of plastic containers from going to the landfill. To further reduce waste, look for bars of soap with minimal packaging.

An alternative to this idea that works better for me is:

_____

_____

October 29

Plan your route for trick-or-treating.

Instead of driving across town, go door-to-door in your own neighborhood. You'll reduce your carbon footprint (and keep pint-size trick-or-treaters safe) by walking, not driving, on Halloween.

An alternative to this idea that works better for me is:

October 30

Buy Halloween treats with recyclable packaging.

The wrappers from mini chocolate bars have to be tossed in the trash, but little cardboard boxes filled with jellybeans and chocolates can be recycled. You could also give out cans of soda; the aluminum cans can be recycled after the little ghosts and goblins are finished.

Americans spend $21 million on Halloween candy every year—more than on Easter and Valentine's Day combined

An alternative to this idea that works better for me is:
_____
_____

October 31

Turn out the lights.

Halloween is supposed to be scary, so use it as an excuse to conserve energy. The average household spends 11 percent of its energy budget on lighting. Keep the porch light on to welcome trick-or-treaters and use candlelight inside the house to set the mood. Send your little trick-or-treaters out with glow sticks or LED flashlights; it'll help set a spooky mood on Halloween night.

> Decorate your house with natural materials like hay bales and cornstalks (which can be composted or added to the garden for mulch after Halloween) instead of using store-bought decorations, which often travel thousands of miles before reaching store shelves.

An alternative to this idea that works better for me is:
_____
_____

November 1

Think twice before tossing your jack-o-lantern in the trash.

Your Halloween pumpkin can provide a feast for wildlife. Smash the pumpkin into chunks and scatter the pieces in the backyard. The birds and squirrels will feast on the seeds and pumpkin flesh. Put any leftover pieces in your compost pile.

An alternative to this idea that works better for me is:

_____

_____

November 2

Test your home for radon.

Radon is a radioactive gas that is created when the uranium in soil and water breaks down and is released into the air. It can seep into your home through cracks in the walls and floors, gaps around pipes, and construction joints. Radon levels can be especially high during the winter months when your windows and doors are closed.

> According to the EPA, 1 in every 15 homes in the United States has unacceptably high radon levels. Radon exposure is responsible for up to 22,000 cancer deaths every year.

Radon test kits are available at home improvement stores for around $20. If the radon levels in your home are too high (the EPA considers radon levels of more than 4 picoCuries per liter unacceptable), there are kits to help you reduce the radon level in your home by up to 99 percent.

You can learn more about radon testing at www.epa.gov/iaq/radon.

An alternative to this idea that works better for me is:

November 3

Replace incandescent light bulbs with compact florescent bulbs (CFLs).

The end of daylight savings time means the lights are on longer; replace your incandescent bulbs now and you'll benefit from the energy savings all winter long. CFLs use 75 percent less energy, last up to 10 times longer, and can save approximately $30 in energy costs over the life of the bulb.

> Replacing one incandescent light bulb with a compact florescent bulb in every home in America would save $600 million in annual energy costs; prevent greenhouse gases equivalent to the emissions of 800,000 cars; and save enough energy to light more than 3 million homes for an entire year.

An alternative to this idea that works better for me is:

_____

_____

November 4

Install motion sensors outside your home.

Now that you've replaced the incandescent bulbs throughout the house, it's time to make a green adjustment to your outdoor lighting. Motion sensors only turn on when there is movement—like someone walking up to your door—and turn off automatically. You'll have the benefit of added security around your home, and you'll never use too much energy because you forgot to turn off your outdoor lights.

An alternative to this idea that works better for me is:

November 5

Think about ways to make your next skiing/snowboarding trip more eco-friendly.

It's time to hit the slopes! Almost 13 million Americans go skiing and snowboarding every winter. You can minimize your impact on the environment by carpooling to the slopes and staying on marked trails. Hitting virgin terrain could damage fragile ecosystems and disturb wildlife, so stick to the trails the resort has groomed for skiers and snowboarders.

An alternative to this idea that works better for me is:

_____

_____

November 6

Ask about teleconferencing at the office.

You could drive across town—or fly across the country—to meet with a client, or you could schedule a conference call. Conference calls cost a fraction of site-to-site travel and save a significant amount of energy. Replacing one cross-country trip with a conference call saves 0.4 metric tons of carbon and enough energy to power 7,000 hours of videoconferences.

An alternative to this idea that works better for me is:

_____

_____

November 7

Think twice before putting garbage in the fire-place.

It's okay to use old newspapers to start a fire, but plastic, fabric, and metal should never be burned. You could be releasing toxic pollutants into the atmosphere by burning nonwood products. Make sure that the wood you're burning is not painted or treated with other chemicals that could be harmful to the environment.

An alternative to this idea that works better for me is:
_____
_____

November 8

Check the hose behind your washing machine.

A kinked hose is more likely to crack and leak. Even a few tiny cracks can lead to a lot of wasted water—and possible water damage. Your washing machine will also use more energy pushing water through a kinked hose. Look behind the washing machine; if the hose is kinked, take a few minutes to straighten it out. If the hose is cracked, buy a new one from the local home improvement store.

An alternative to this idea that works better for me is:

November 9

Shop for an extra-large bag of pet food.

You could drive to the pet store every weekend to buy a five-pound bag of food for Fido or Fluffy. Or you could buy a 30-pound bag and save your Saturday mornings for playing with your four-legged friend. Buying pet food in bulk has the same advantages as buying bulk goods at the supermarket—it cuts down on packaging waste and trips to the store. Bulk pet food is often less expensive, too. If you feed your pets canned food, be sure to recycle the metal cans.

An alternative to this idea that works better for me is:
_____
_____

November 10

Check your pilot lights.

Gas appliances like the stove, fireplace, and furnace all have pilot lights. The flame will be blue if the appliance is working efficiently. If the flame is yellow or red, it's time to call the gas company to have the appliance serviced. The more efficiently your gas appliances work, the more energy you'll save.

An alternative to this idea that works better for me is:
_____
_____

November 11

Start filling your freezer.

Your refrigerator and freezer are responsible for about one sixth of the energy use in your home—more than any other single household appliance.

You can help your freezer run more efficiently by keeping it full. The more frozen items that are in your freezer, the less space there is to trap warm air when the door is opened. When warm air enters your freezer, it has to work harder to maintain its temperature.

Can't afford to stock up on frozen items this week? Fill a few plastic jugs with water and store them in the freezer; the frozen masses will help the freezer run more efficiently when the door is opened.

An alternative to this idea that works better for me is:

_____

_____

November 12

Think twice before flushing the toilet.

Each time you flush, you use up to six gallons of water. You probably don't need to flush the toilet every time you go to the bathroom—often called the "if it's yellow, let it mellow" rule. Skipping just one flush per day will save up to 1,460 gallons of water per year!

An alternative to this idea that works better for me is:

_____

_____

November 13

Research options for recycling your old MP3 player.

Before you buy a new MP3 player, recycle the old one. Close to 40 percent of all of the lead in U.S. landfills comes from electronic waste.

Instead of tossing your old MP3 player in the trash, where the lead can cause toxic pollution of the air and groundwater, see whether the manufacturer will recycle it. Some manufacturers, such as Apple, will give you a 10 percent discount off the purchase of a new MP3 player when you bring in your old one to recycle.

An alternative to this idea that works better for me is:

_____

_____

November 14

Try a new type of fish.

Buy (or order) wild seafood instead of farmed varieties. Farmed fish have higher levels of heavy metal and generate a lot of waste because they live in such a tightly packed environment. In fact, the average fish farm releases the same amount of nitrogen, phosphorous, and waste as a small town.

An alternative to this idea that works better for me is:

_____

_____

November 15

Check your windows.

Now that cooler temperatures have arrived, make sure your windows are closed tightly. Heat will disappear out the windows if they're left open, even if it's just a crack. Take a few minutes to go from room to room to double-check that heat isn't escaping outside through an open window. You'll cut your energy costs dramatically and keep your home comfortable all winter long.

An alternative to this idea that works better for me is:

_____

_____

November 16

Research your options for energy-efficient home-office equipment.

When the time comes to buy new home-office equipment, you could buy a printer, copier, scanner, and a fax machine, or you could opt for an all-in-one unit. Using one multitasking machine instead of a different piece of equipment for every task can save almost 200 kWh of energy per year—not to mention the space it'll save in your office. Depending on your needs, you can find one for under $100 at office-supply stores.

An alternative to this idea that works better for me is:

_____

_____

November 17

DONE ○

Measure the water in your tea kettle.

You don't need to boil eight cups of water to brew a single mug of tea. The more water you put in your kettle, the more energy it takes to boil. By boiling only as much water as you need, you'll cut down on water waste and save energy.

> Don't put water in the microwave to boil. There are some safety concerns associated with microwaving water; go to www.fda.gov/cdrh/consumer/microwave.html for information.

An alternative to this idea that works better for me is:

_____

_____

November 18

Ease up when you step on the gas.

Resist the urge to stomp on the accelerator when the light turns green. Accelerating gradually uses a lot less gas than putting the pedal to the metal. You'll improve your fuel efficiency by up to 20 percent if you accelerate slowly.

An alternative to this idea that works better for me is:

_____

_____

November 19

Choose chlorine-free feminine hygiene products.

Most of the tampons and pads on store shelves are bleached with chlorine, which leaches into the groundwater during the manufacturing process. Once these products reach the landfill, the chlorine ends up in the soil. You can find chlorine-free feminine hygiene products at most supermarkets and natural-products retailers—just look for products labeled "chlorine-free."

An alternative to this idea that works better for me is:
_____
_____

November 20

Polish your silver with natural ingredients.

Conventional silver polish contains harsh chemicals such as ammonia. There are natural alternatives to get your best silver to sparkle for Thanksgiving dinner.

To clean a few small pieces of silver, use a dab of white toothpaste. Squeeze a drop of toothpaste on your finger and rub it onto the silver for instant polish. If you have a lot of silver to polish, boil a few strips of aluminum foil and two tablespoons of baking soda in a pan. Add your silverware and let it sit for a few minutes to remove the tarnish.

An alternative to this idea that works better for me is:

_____

_____

November 21

Use your PDA or cell phone to send short messages.

Need to remind your spouse to pick up a gallon of milk on the way home? Send a text message instead of an e-mail. Text messages use 30 times less energy than sending an e-mail from a desktop computer. Use your cell phone or PDA to send the same message with less impact on the environment.

An alternative to this idea that works better for me is:
_____
_____

November 22

Cancel duplicate magazine subscriptions.

Are there multiple copies of the same trade magazine floating around your office? Your co-workers probably get a few of the same magazines you do. Cancel your subscription and encourage your officemates to share their issues.

An alternative to this idea that works better for me is:

_____

_____

November 23

Contact the post office to stop the mail before you go on holidays.

The U.S. Postal Service delivers 212 billion pieces of mail every year. The cost of transporting all of those letters adds up. You can help the post office cut down on transportation costs by stopping mail delivery while you're away.

An alternative to this idea that works better for me is:

_____

_____

November 24

Stock up on fresh veggies.

It takes 3 *billion* kWh of energy per year to produce canned vegetables—enough energy to run 8,571,428 refrigerators for an entire year! Instead of frozen or canned vegetables, choose fresh potatoes and yams for Thanksgiving dinner.

An alternative to this idea that works better for me is:

_____

_____

November 25

Ask guests to bring reusable to-go containers to Thanksgiving dinner.

You'll probably have lots of leftover turkey and mashed potatoes. Every year, Americans use enough plastic wrap to cover all of Texas. Instead of sending your guests home with leftovers piled on paper plates and covered in plastic wrap, ask them to bring their own to-go containers.

An alternative to this idea that works better for me is:

_____

_____

November 26

Invest in a roasting pan.

Disposable roasting pans are inexpensive and readily available on grocery store shelves, especially at this time of year. But if everyone in the United States used a disposable roasting pan to cook their Thanksgiving turkey, there would be 46 million tinfoil pans heading to the landfill every year. Instead, buy a heavy-duty roasting pan that you can use every Thanksgiving (or any time you feel like cooking a turkey or a roast). Consider it an investment in the environment.

An alternative to this idea that works better for me is:

_____

_____

November 27

Let leftovers cool before refrigerating them.

Putting in containers filled with piping-hot mashed potatoes, gravy, and leftover turkey will decrease the efficiency of your refrigerator. The steam will raise the temperature in the refrigerator, causing it to work harder to stay cool. Enjoy an extra slice of pumpkin pie and wait until your leftovers cool before putting them in the refrigerator.

> Don't let leftovers sit out too long. Bacteria can grow on certain foods (especially dishes made with meat and eggs) if they're left at room temperature for extended periods, so don't wait too long before putting leftovers in the refrigerator.

An alternative to this idea that works better for me is:

_____

_____

November 28

Learn to make turkey stock.

Don't let your Thanksgiving turkey go to waste. Use the remains to make stock for turkey soup. Simply boil the turkey carcass in a pot of water with carrots, onions, celery, and salt until the stock turns golden brown. Add pieces of left-over turkey and serve piping hot. It's one of the most delicious ways to reduce, reuse, and recycle.

An alternative to this idea that works better for me is:

_____

_____

November 29

Buy a salad spinner.

Stop drying your lettuce on piles of paper towel! A salad spinner is an inexpensive and waste-free way to remove all of the moisture from your salad greens. After you've removed the lettuce from the salad spinner, pour the leftover water on your favorite houseplants.

An alternative to this idea that works better for me is:

_____

_____

November 30

Plan one big holiday party.

Let family and friends know that your Christmas gift to the planet is a smaller carbon footprint and suggest a single holiday party. Make plans to get together on one day to celebrate the season.

It might take a little more planning to host a single gathering, but the impact on the environment will be huge: if 20 people in every state cut out a 10-mile car trip once a week, it would prevent more than 64,000 pounds of pollutants from being released into the air.

No matter how many holiday parties you attend this season, be sure to carpool.

An alternative to this idea that works better for me is:

_____

_____

December 1

Take inventory of your holiday décor.

Do you need a festive serving bowl or a new stocking for your mantle? Make a list of the things you need and look for them at secondhand stores. At this time of year, the aisles of thrift shops are filled with gently used holiday decorations. You'll find all the things you need to trim your tree at a fraction of the price and help keep boxes of ornaments and other items from going to the landfill.

An alternative to this idea that works better for me is:

_____

_____

December 2

Go online to check the proofs of your holiday card photos.

If sending holiday cards with a family photo is a tradition, look at the photos electronically before ordering. You'll cut out the use of chemical inks and heavy-duty photo paper if you view the proofs online.

Once you've picked the photo for your holiday cards, be sure to order only as many cards as you plan to send to eliminate waste.

An alternative to this idea that works better for me is:

_____

_____

December 3

Send your holiday greetings electronically.

Almost 2.65 billion Christmas cards are sold in the United States every year—enough cards to circle the planet 10 times! Sending electronic holiday cards is a simple way to reduce the amount of holiday waste.

Websites such as www.hallmark.com and www.photobucket.com offer a selection of holiday e-cards that can be personalized and sent to family and friends.

> If you prefer the more traditional route of sending holiday cards through the mail, look for cards printed on recycled paper with soy-based ink.

An alternative to this idea that works better for me is:

_____

_____

December 4

Order LED holiday lights.

Most retailers stock energy-efficient holiday lights made with light-emitting diodes, or LEDs. LED lights are 90 percent more efficient than traditional Christmas lights and last longer—up to 10,000 hours compared with 5,000 hours for incandescent bulbs.

> You can increase your energy savings with solar lights. Retailers like www.gaiam.com sell strands of LED lights with solar panels that don't require any electrical connection. Holiday wreaths and decorative icicles are also available with solar panels.

An alternative to this idea that works better for me is:

_____

_____

December 5

Think green when making your holiday shopping list.

You can green your holiday shopping by choosing gifts that are eco-friendly, shopping at locally owned stores, or buying from retailers who use a portion of their profits to support environmental causes.

A 2007 holiday shopping survey by KPMG found that 88 percent of respondents were concerned about the environment. Almost three quarters of shoppers buy eco-friendly products and 55 percent made a special effort to patronize retailers with a reputation for being green.

An alternative to this idea that works better for me is:

DONE
○

December 6

Put your holiday lights on timers.

Leaving your holiday lights turned on 24 hours a day will quadruple your energy costs—and create four times the pollution—as leaving them on for six hours. Set your timer to turn the lights on at dusk and leave them on until you go to bed. You'll be able to enjoy the lights all evening without burning energy overnight.

An alternative to this idea that works better for me is:

December 7

Make a list of must-have green gifts.

Be prepared when someone asks, "What do you want for Christmas?" Ask for eco-friendly gifts like organic wine and fair-trade handicrafts. Or ask for a donation to be made in your name to a charity that supports environmental causes.

An alternative to this idea that works better for me is:

_____

_____

December 8

Rethink your holiday wardrobe.

The invitation to your office holiday party requests "formal attire." You can look your best without spending a fortune on a dress you'll only wear once. Ask a same-size friend if she has a formal dress you can borrow. Not an option? Buy a dress from a consignment shop. Consignment shops only accept the latest fashions in perfect condition. You'll spend a fraction of the money to "recycle" a dress. Bonus: you can put it back on consignment at the shop where you purchased it. (Be sure to take it to an eco-friendly dry cleaner first.)

An alternative to this idea that works better for me is:

_____

_____

December 9

DONE
○

Make plans to carpool to a Hanukkah party.

Call family and friends and suggest going to a Hanukkah party together, instead of driving separately. Or call an elderly member of your synagogue and offer to pick her up for nightly services. You'll reduce your carbon footprint and help spread the spirit of the season.

An alternative to this idea that works better for me is:
_____
_____

December 10

Decorate with natural materials.

You can make beautiful holiday decorations with items found in nature: a bowl of evergreen boughs and fresh fruit, a basket filled with fallen branches, winter berries, and pinecones, and seasonal plants like poinsettias make inexpensive holiday décor. Once the holidays are over, your decorations can be added to the compost pile.

> Holiday plants like poinsettias and mistletoe are toxic to pets. Opt for more pet-friendly greenery (think evergreen boughs and pine cones) or display toxic plants out of reach of your pets.

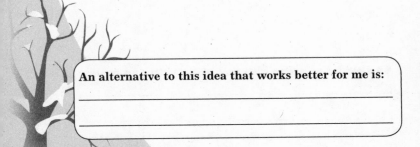

An alternative to this idea that works better for me is:

_____

_____

December 11

Use an inherited menorah to celebrate Hanukkah.

You could buy a brand-new menorah or you could light candles in the same menorah that has been in your family for generations. Not only will an inherited menorah have special meaning, it'll save you from driving to the store to buy a new one.

> Make your Hanukkah celebra-
> tions even more eco-friendly by
> using soy-based candles in your
> menorah. Soy candles are made
> from renewable resources and
> last twice as long as conven-
> tional paraffin candles.

An alternative to this idea that works better for me is:

_____

_____

DONE

December 12

Start gathering eco-friendly packing materials.

Mail your holiday gifts in boxes padded with recycled newspaper or shredded paper. You can also use real peanuts and include a note asking the recipient to feed them to the squirrels once the box is unpacked. These green materials will protect your packages just as well as bubble wrap or Styrofoam but have none of the negative impacts on the environment.

> Styrofoam accounts for up to 25 percent of the waste in our landfills. When it's burned, Styrofoam releases over 90 different toxins including dioxin, a known carcinogen.

An alternative to this idea that works better for me is:

_____

_____

December 13

Buy a cut Christmas tree.

Nearly all cut Christmas trees were grown on tree farms, which means their stock is replenished yearly and forests aren't depleted. Cut trees are a much greener choice than artificial trees, which are made with petroleum-based materials and often shipped thousands of miles before they reach your living room.

Unlike artificial trees, which eventually end up in the landfill, cut trees can be recycled after the holidays (see January 1).

An alternative to this idea that works better for me is:

December 14

Wrap presents in gift bags.

Once you tear the wrapping paper off of a holiday gift it ends up in the recycle bin, but gift bags can be used over and over again.

Use the comics section of the newspaper, outdated maps, or paper grocery bags to wrap gifts. You can also look for gift bags made with recycled content or purchase plain paper bags and decorate them yourself with recycled holiday cards.

If every family in the United States reused two feet of holiday ribbon, it would save 38,000 miles of ribbon—enough to tie a bow around the entire planet.

An alternative to this idea that works better for me is:

_____

_____

December 15

Shop for holiday gifts that don't require batteries.

Nearly 40 percent of all battery sales occur during the holidays. Eventually, worn-out batteries end up in the landfill where they leach toxic metals into the soil and groundwater. Call your local waste-management company to find out how to dispose of batteries in your area—don't just throw them in the trash.

You can help keep batteries from going to the landfill by choosing holiday gifts that don't require batteries. If you do buy gifts that require batteries, give rechargeable batteries.

An alternative to this idea that works better for me is:

December 16

Remove the snow and ice from your car.

The snow that piles up on the hood, roof, and windows can be very heavy. Taking a few minutes to scrape snow and ice off your car will help improve your vehicle's fuel efficiency and make your drive safer.

It might be tempting to let your car run while you're scraping (the heat will help it melt a little faster) but an idling engine is a major source of pollution. Invest in a good-quality scraper and snow brush and wait until you're ready to leave the house before starting the car.

An alternative to this idea that works better for me is:

December 17

Buy shares in an eco-friendly company.

If you need to buy a holiday gift for the person who has everything, consider giving him or her shares in a company with an environmental mission. It's a gift that will keep on giving—to the recipient and the environment.

An alternative to this idea that works better for me is:
_____
_____

December 18

Create a homemade garland for the Christmas tree.

An old-fashioned string of popcorn and cranberries will look great on your tree. Once the holidays are over, you can hang the garland in an evergreen tree in your backyard and let the birds feast on your creation.

An alternative to this idea that works better for me is:

_____

_____

December 19

Buy reusable containers for homemade treats.

Batches of sugar cookies, homemade preserves, and rum-soaked fruitcake are perfect holiday gifts for friends and neighbors. Be sure to package them in festive holiday tins. Unlike paper plates or cardboard boxes, which will end up in the recycle bin (or the trash), tins can be used over and over again.

An alternative to this idea that works better for me is:

December 20

Pack light for holiday travel.

Excess weight in the trunk of your car (or in the cargo hold on the plane) will decrease your gas mileage. In the car, every 100 pounds of cargo decreases fuel efficiency by 2 percent. It might not sound like much, but it adds up on a round-trip to visit relatives; so only pack the essentials.

An alternative to this idea that works better for me is:

December 21

Pay a teenager to shovel your driveway.

You could go outside and do it yourself or you could help one of the teenagers in your neighborhood earn some spending money. Shoveling the driveway by hand is also better for the environment. Research shows that small gasoline engines, like those used in snow blowers, produce the same amount of pollution as a car.

> Calculate the amount of pollution that your snow blower produces by going to www.etc-cte.ec.gc.ca/databases/snowbloweremissions and entering some basic information.

An alternative to this idea that works better for me is:

December 22

Stock up on local holiday ales.

Serve beer that was made at local microbreweries. In the United States, adults drink
about 6.5 billion gallons of beer per year. You'll
be supporting a locally owned business and can
help cut down on fossil fuel consumption by
buying beer that was brewed close to home. Look
for special-edition holiday ales made by many
microbreweries.

An alternative to this idea that works better for me is:
_____
_____

December 23

Make a holiday coupon book.

· Holiday sales in the United States total more than $200 billion per year. Instead of going to the mall to shop for mass-produced holiday gifts, make your own. Make a book filled with coupons for thoughtful gifts like a candlelit dinner, a back-rub, or complete control of the remote for an entire evening.

An alternative to this idea that works better for me is:

_____

_____

December 24

Set out treats for Santa.

A glass of soy milk and a plate of homemade chocolate chip cookies will give Santa the energy to continue his around-the-world trip. Don't forget to leave a bunch of organic carrots and apples for his reindeer—it takes a lot of energy to power a sleigh!

An alternative to this idea that works better for me is:

December 25

Make a vegetarian dish for your holiday dinner.

Along with a traditional Christmas feast of turkey and stuffing, prepare vegetarian dishes like candied sweet potatoes, creamed carrots, and mushroom gravy. Eating vegetarian dishes will help reduce your carbon footprint and prevent air and water pollution.

Feeling daring? Make tofurkey! This turkey look-alike is made from soy protein and has less impact on the environment than a farm-raised bird. You just might start a new holiday tradition.

> It takes approximately 2,500 gallons of water to raise one pound of beef. In contrast, growing one pound of soy requires 250 gallons of water and it takes just 25 gallons of water to grow one pound of wheat.

An alternative to this idea that works better for me is:

_____

_____

December 26

Plan an eco-friendly Kwanzaa celebration.

Celebrate the values of family, community, commerce, and self-improvement while honoring the environment, too. Choose an antique kinara (candleholder), use soy candles, and shop at local retailers for fair-trade handicrafts, items made from recycled materials, and other gifts that have minimal impact on the planet.

An alternative to this idea that works better for me is:

_____

_____

December 27

Skip post-holiday shopping.

Instead of getting in the car, driving to the mall, and waiting in long lines to buy holiday décor at clearance prices, start a new tradition: spend the day at home with loved ones. You'll reduce fuel consumption and avoid cluttering your home and garage with mass-produced goods.

An alternative to this idea that works better for me is:

_____

_____

December 28

Save your holiday cards.

The greetings you got this year don't have to go in the recycle bin. Instead, save them to make gift tags for the gifts you'll give next year.

An alternative to this idea that works better for me is:
_____
_____

December 29

Buy artificial fire logs.

In most cases, natural products are almost always the greener option, but that's not the case when it comes to starting a fire.

Artificial fire logs emit 75 percent less carbon monoxide and create 80 percent less particulate matter than real wood. The faux fireplace logs are also more efficient at heating your home than real wood, giving off up to 15,190 BTU per pound compared with 8,300 BTU per pound for oak.

An alternative to this idea that works better for me is:

_____

_____

December 30

Stock up on sand to prevent slippery sidewalks.

Salt might make the ice melt, but it's harmful to the environment (not to mention your pet's paws). Excess salt can kill trees and increases the acidity of water. It also attracts wildlife such as deer to the roadways, causing collisions with cars.

Sand is a salt- and chemical-free alternative that's just as effective for preventing your driveway, porch, and sidewalks from becoming too slippery.

An alternative to this idea that works better for me is:

_____

_____

December 31

Make a New Year's resolution to be even more eco-friendly next year.

What steps can you take to further reduce your impact on the earth next year? Plan in advance for big projects like installing solar panels or establishing a green roof. Be sure to make a toast to congratulate yourself for all of the changes you made this year!

An alternative to this idea that works better for me is:

_____

_____

Resources

Books

Davis, Brangien, and Katherine Wroth, eds. *Wake Up and Smell the Planet: The Non-Pompous, Non-Preachy Grist Guide to Greening Your Day*. Mountaineers Books, 2007.

Dorfman, Josh. *The Lazy Environmentalist: Your Guide to Easy, Stylish, Green Living*. Stewart, Tabori & Chang, 2007.

Riley, Trish. *The Complete Idiot's Guide to Green Living*. Alpha Books, 2007.

Trask, Crissy. *It's Easy Being Green: A Handbook for Earth-Friendly Living*. Gibbs Smith, 2006.

Websites

http://sierraclub.typepad.com/greenlife
The nonprofit Sierra Club publishes a blog with the latest news and trends on the environmental front.

www.americanwater.com/49ways.htm
Log on for a wealth of water-saving tips from American Water and Energy Savers.

www.ase.org   The Alliance to Save Energy website has information about why it's important to save energy and how you can do your part to cut down on energy consumption.

www.eere.energy.gov   The U.S. Department of Energy Efficiency and Renewable Energy website is filled with information on the strides that are being made in this area.

www.grist.org   Check this website for an online magazine featuring articles about environmental topics.

www.thegreenguide.com   A companion to the print edition of the *National Geographic Green Guide*, this website is filled with articles and information about environmental topics.

www.treehugger.com   Check this website for an online news magazine for green-minded readers.

www.wateruseitwisely.com   Part of the Water—Use it Wisely campaign, this website offers lots of water-saving tips and activities.

Magazines

E, the Environmental Magazine
www.emagazine.com
1-800-967-6572

National Geographic
www.nationalgeographic.com
1-800-647-5463

Orion
www.orionmagazine.org
1-800-254-3713

Plenty Magazine
www.plentymag.com
1-800-316-9006